THE IRISH

THE IRISH ECONOMY

Results and Prospects

RONNIE MUNCK

Pluto **Press**

LONDON • BOULDER, COLORADO

First Published 1993 by Pluto Press
345 Archway Road, London N6 5AA
and 5500 Central Avenue
Boulder, Colorado 80301, USA

British Library Cataloguing in Publication Data
A catalogue record for this book is available from
the British Library
ISBN 0 7453 0673 X hb
ISBN 0 7453 0674 8 pb

Library of Congress Cataloging in Publication Data
Munck, Ronaldo.
    The Irish economy : results and prospects / Ronnie Munck.
        p.   cm.
    Includes bibliographical references and index.
    ISBN 0-7453-0673-X. – ISBN 0-7453-0674-8 (pbk.)
    1. Ireland–Economic conditions. 2. Northern Ireland–Economic
conditions. 3. Agriculture–Economic aspects–Ireland. 4. European Economic
Community–Ireland.
HC260.5.M86 1993
330.9415–DC20   92-45632
                                                 CIP

Produced for Pluto Press by
Chase Production Services, Chipping Norton
Typeset in 10 on 12 pt Times by Archetype
Printed in Finland by WSOY

Contents

Tables and Figures

Tables

Figures

Foreword

The economic developments now occurring in Ireland, and more generally Europe, raise difficult questions and challenge many long-held beliefs. Discussion of these issues has been rather limited up to now, especially in Northern Ireland, but over the coming years the debate is certain to intensify. Ronnie Munck's book, *The Irish Economy: Results and Prospects*, is a valuable contribution to this debate. Its author is well-versed in Third World theories of economic development, such as dependency theory, and he uses this knowledge to explore the economic history of Ireland and analyse the problems now facing the island. This makes the book unusual in both approach and sweep, and for this reason alone it is valuable. The author writes from a radical perspective, but he is undogmatic and the general tenor of the book is open-minded. This book should be useful to anyone seriously interested in the Irish economy no matter what their political views. I have certainly enjoyed reading it and I am sure others will too.

The partition of Ireland occurred seventy years ago. This event damaged the economy of the island and inhibited future development. It disrupted trade flows between North and South and weakened the already somewhat tenuous economic links between the two regions. More fundamentally, partition cemented political divisions in Ireland and prevented the formation of a sense of common purpose and determination to overcome the island's economic backwardness.

The two parts of Ireland have been affected somewhat differently by partition. In its early years, the economic development of the South was inhibited by its separation from the industrially more advanced North, whose skilled workforce and entrepreneurs could have contributed a great deal to a united Ireland. For its part, the North has suffered because of its overdependence on Britain, which in recent years has brought considerable benefit in the form of financial subsidies, but has simultaneously reduced the region's capacity for self-sustaining economic development. Personal incomes and the standard of living are, on average, higher in the North than the South, but this is entirely because of the huge subsidies which the region receives from Britain. These subsidies provide employment and shore up living standards in the North, but in doing so they create attitudes and incentives which inhibit economic regeneration.

Economic development in the South has been more impressive than in the North, especially over the past twenty years, and the Southern economy is now much stronger than its Northern counterpart. Without the huge subsidies it receives from Britain, the Northern economy would simply collapse. The South gets some financial support from the European Community, but the amount is relatively small and its withdrawal would be a painful, but not fatal blow. For all its faults, the South is now an independent and self-supporting economic entity, whilst the North is a dependent client of the British state.

Economic development in the South has gone through several phases since partition. After initial hesitation, the South pursued a classic import substitution strategy, based on the idea of building up home industries behind a tariff wall and increasing self-sufficiency. To some degree, this path was forced on the country during the interwar period by external economic and political events, including the world recession and the Anglo-Irish trade war. It was also in line with the doctrine of self-sufficiency which the De Valera government inherited from Sinn Fein. For a time this inward-looking strategy was tolerably successful, but by the 1950s its potential was clearly exhausted. In 1958 it was replaced by a radically new strategy of converting Ireland into an export base for foreign multinationals. This had both positive and negative sides. It attracted a large amount of foreign investment into modern industries, and to this extent was successful. However, it was accompanied by a prolonged decline in many traditional industries and by a failure to develop new indigenous firms in the modern sector. As a result, despite considerable foreign investment, the economy of the South remains both fragile and inadequate. It is fragile because of the weakness of domestic producers and the region's overdependence on outside multinationals. Its inadequacy is reflected in the South's persistent failure to provide anything remotely approaching full employment. Of all countries in the OECD, the Irish Republic has the worst record for employment growth over the past decade and currently has the second highest rate of unemployment.

At the time of partition, the Northern economy was a world leader in shipbuilding and linen, and the economic future of the region appeared secure. But this strength was deceptive since both industries were vulnerable to competition from foreign producers or rival products. Soon after partition, these industries went into a long-term decline, which was interrupted for a time by the Second World War and its aftermath, but resumed once again as normal world trading conditions were restored during the 1950s. The government of Northern Ireland responded to this decline by seeking to attract outside investment to the region. Generous financial incentives were given to outside investors with the aim of converting the North into an export base for multinationals. This policy was at first successful and for some years the Northern economy grew rapidly. But it suffered from a crucial weakness. Local industries were neglected and the once impressive entrepreneurial capacities of the North were allowed to atrophy. This left the region highly dependent on the goodwill and priorities of outside multinationals. In the 1970s, the North was hit by the twin blows of guerrilla warfare at home and the onset of European economic stagnation. Many of the original multinational investors in Northern Ireland have closed down their operations, whilst new investment from outside is now only a trickle. The precise role of the conflict in these developments is difficult to determine. Few multinationals have closed down their operations in Northern Ireland simply because of the conflict. Most closures seem to have been motivated by global economic considerations and would have occurred even under normal conditions. But the conflict has almost certainly been a major deterrent to new investors. Under present day economic conditions, why should multinational firms take the risk of coming to Northern Ireland, when they can take their pick from dozens of cheap, high unemployment locations elsewhere in Europe, including, of course, the Irish Republic?

Both North and South are now at an impasse. The South has attracted a great deal of outside investment, but this has not been sufficient to offset the decline of indigenous producers. The result has been widespread unemployment and poverty. The North is in an even weaker situation since it now receives very little outside investment and is shored up by massive financial support from Great Britain. In both North and South, there is a growing awareness that such extreme dependence on outside resources is undesirable, because it makes the regions concerned so vulnerable to external events. It is also not a viable route to prosperity. Few would seriously argue that outside investment or financial support should be rejected or even drastically cut back. But there is an increasing recognition that something more is required. To overcome their present difficulties, the Irish people, North and South, must rely more on themselves. They must take the future into their own hands. The development of indigenous firms must be encouraged in both traditional and modern industries, whilst the education and skills of the local workforce must be enhanced at all levels. The aim cannot be a return to the old ideal of self-sufficiency which would be utterly impractical under modern conditions. On the contrary, the aim must be to increase the volume of goods and services exported, and this must be done by creating a vigorous and flexible network of locally controlled firms serving the world market. Without such a network Ireland, North and South, will remain both relatively poor and highly vulnerable to external events. Economic independence cannot be achieved by cutting oneself off from the outside world, but by developing a strong, indigenous export sector with the ability to respond flexibly and creatively to shifts in the world market.

The need to develop and strengthen indigenous industry is now recognised throughout Ireland and government policies are shifting in this direction. This has been the official line in the North for some time, which is hardly surprising given the difficulty of attracting outside investment in recent years. Government policy in the South is also beginning to emphasise the importance of indigenous producers, and the publication of the Culliton Report in 1992 is likely to accelerate this trend.

Alongside the new emphasis on indigenous industry, there has been a marked upsurge in the extent of economic cooperation between North and South. The impetus for this has come primarily from the private sector and there are now regular North–South contacts between business organisations of all types. This is a recent development for which a major catalyst has been the prospect of the Single European Market and the possibility of monetary union in the future. Closer European integration will provide new opportunities for Irish business but it will also pose new threats. Foreign competitors will find it easier to enter Irish markets, whilst Irish firms may find their peripheral location an even greater disadvantage that at present. Whatever the exact balance between threats and opportunities, it is clear that Irish firms will have to become significantly more competitive in the years ahead, and it is the awareness of this which is causing private business to embrace North–South cooperation so enthusiastically. There is also been a growth in official cooperation between the two areas. The Anglo-Irish Intergovernmental Conference has set up a working group devoted specifically to the subject of North–South economic cooperation, and the two governments are clearly anxious to promote such cooperation.

The political implications of North–South economic cooperation are not yet clear. Some nationalists believe the experience of cooperation will erode the political hostility of Northern unionists and pave the way to the eventual re-unification of Ireland. Some hard-line unionists share their beliefs and therefore oppose cooperation. Sceptics dismiss these hopes and fears as unfounded. They argue that 'technocratic integration' is quite compatible with existing political structures and has few long-term political implications. Personally, I think they are wrong. Extensive North–South cooperation may not lead to painless re-unification as the optimists hope, but in the long run it is bound to soften the attitudes of Northern unionists and improve the prospects for some kind of political settlement. There is also a growing awareness that the Irish people are all in the same boat and must cooperate to survive in the present hostile economic environment.

The process of economic cooperation now developing in Ireland raises a number of questions. Can this process achieve its full potential within the existing institutional and political framework? Or will significant changes be required at some stage in the future? If so, what are these changes? There is also the question of democratic account-ability to consider. There is already a 'democratic deficit' in the North, where the local population has little influence over economic policy which is controlled from Westminster. Intergovernmental cooperation between Britain and the Irish Republic may reinforce this situation in the North, whilst reducing the degree of accountability in the South. There is a danger that the process of cooperation will be dominated by private business interests and popular institutions such as trade unions will be marginalised. This danger is, of course, just an Irish aspect of a more serious problem throughout the European Community, where economic integration is undermining existing democratic institutions. The European Parliament is weak and there are no effective Com-munity-wide institutions which can exert effective democratic control over the integration process or over European economic policy. On a more modest scale the same problem arises in the case of Ireland. Economic cooperation and integration between North and South will have significant implications for both areas, and it is desirable that they be subject to democratic control by those effected, which they are not at present.

Bob Rowthorn
Cambridge University

Acknowledgements

Since this book was completed the Irish economy continues to be in the headlines. The impact of European economic unification is making itself felt in a profound restructuring of the local economy. Prominent business leaders have, also, begun to argue for a view of the Irish economy as a single regional unit. Reports from economic research bodies, both north and south of the border, have, for their part, stressed the need for an alternative economic strategy. Taken together, these tendencies reinforce the approach taken in this book which, at the time of writing, seemed a bit in advance of its time.

I would like to thank Bob Rowthorn not only for providing an illuminating Foreword but also for meticulously reading through the first draft and suggesting useful amendments. Douglas Hamilton not only wrote much of the final chapter but also commented intelligently on the whole text. Trutz Haase kindly provided the chapter on agriculture on the basis of his own research on the subject. Finally, I would like to thank the University of Ulster Publication Committee which provided generous financial backing for this publishing venture. I hope all the above find the end result some reward for their input.

Ronnie Munck
University of Ulster

'If the Irish people do not control Irish industries, transport, money and the soil of the country, then foreign or domestic capitalists will. And whoever control the wealth of a country and the processes by which wealth is attained control also its government.'

Liam Mellows, Kilmainham Jail, 1992.

'It is a time for change . . . Time to accept that the solutions to our problems lie in our own hands. We need to foster a spirit of self-reliance and a determination to take charge of our future.'

Preface to *Culliton Report*, 1992.

Introduction

Economic affairs are generally deemed the province of the specialist. We are all affected by the economy – indeed our life chances are determined by the economy – but we do not always understand its workings. We know, of course, that inflation is 'a bad thing', we are told that unemployment is 'inevitable', or that 'there is no alternative'. There are, certainly, technical economic discussions of considerable complexity but the basic workings of the economy are simply not that difficult to grasp. This book seeks, therefore, to provide a broad historical overview of the Irish economy, including a consideration of the possible alternatives to the present situation.

The Irish economy consists, of course, of two economies, that of the Republic and that of Northern Ireland. The literature tends to treat them separately, except for the rare comparative study or the specialized consideration of crossborder economic projects. So, why a book on the Irish economy as a whole? I believe that there are both economic and political reasons for this treatment. The impact of 1992 and the single European market will inevitably bring the economies of the two jurisdictions closer together. Indeed, for some time it has made more sense to consider agriculture on an all-Ireland basis rather than subsume the north of Ireland within the United Kingdom. Of course, the north of Ireland is, economically, a part of the UK, but its present situation can only be understood in terms of the history of the Irish economy as a whole. In political terms, the prospect of a reunited Ireland, which still exists in spite of all the problems, means that the two Irish economies should be considered together. Apart from anything else, it allows us to consider whether a united Ireland would in fact be economically viable. So, though the Southern and Northern economies receive separate treatment in the pages that follow, there is a constant concern with the all-Ireland dimension.

Chapter 1 of this work carries out a broad sweep of the Irish economy, from its origins to the partition of Ireland and the emergence of two separate economies in 1921. This chapter also begins to develop the theoretical framework of dependent development, which avoids the pitfalls of simple nationalist economics and the over-optimistic reading of orthodox modernization theory alike. The reasons behind the early industrialization in the North and the de-industrialization of the rest of the country are examined. Particular attention is paid to the causes behind the economic decline of the nineteenth century where no simple explanations are accepted. The chapter ends with a balance-sheet of the whole Irish economy on the eve of partition and the emergence of two separate Irish economies.

Chapter 2 and 3 deal respectively with the Southern and Northern economies from partition to the present. The legacy of colonial domination and partition would affect both economies considerably, if in different ways. A similar pattern of industrialization, based largely on foreign capital, eventually emerged in the 1960s. It is ironic that the two economies have probably become more similar under partition than if a single Irish economy had continued. The prospects of both economies are set, in common terms, by the European Community and integration into the world capitalist economy. However, the North's continued integration with the British economy has become progressively detrimental, compared to the imperialist heyday when the Industrial Revolution spread to that part of Ireland. These chapters provide a sobering balance-sheet of 70 years of economic policy making in the two Irish states.

In orthodox economics workers are relegated to a specialist area known as 'manpower economics': Chapter 4 deals with workers and the economy in a somewhat different spirit. We examine who works where in the two Irish economies, and the distribution of income, the issue of emigration, and the division of workers according to religion and gender. In a sense this chapter is about the effects of the Irish economy on the working population, which is, at the same time, the driving force behind economic development. It is workers in particular who might have an interest in some alternative model of economic development.

Chapter 5 takes up what is known as the agrarian question, examining the political economy of agriculture from the nineteenth century to the present. Once of crucial economic and political significance, agriculture has lost its pre-eminent economic role, but it still has greater importance than in most Western European countries, and considerable political significance, particularly in the South.

Chapter 6 takes up the vital European context and the impact that 1992 and the single market will have on the Irish economy, North and South. Membership of the European Economic Community in 1973 led to a certain 'honeymoon period' especially in agriculture. Now the economic integration implicit in the 1992 measures is seen as a prelude to concentration and rationalization, with its inevitable social corollary of unemployment and poverty. Whether a united Ireland or any other alternative arrangement would have a viable future outside Europe is, of course, a different matter. My own feeling is that this is the context in which all the various economic options – reactionary and progressive alike – will have to be set.

Chapter 7 examines some of these alternative scenarios, exploring the implications of the various options now open to the Irish economies. If previous chapters chronicle the 'results' of the book's title, this final chapter takes up the challenge of the prospects open to it. We start, logically enough, by charting the possible effects of a continuation of present policies. This section thus is a follow-up to the chapters on the Southern (chapter 2) and Northern (chapter 3) economies and that on 1992 (chapter 6). Another scenario to consider in terms of its economic implications is that of an independent Ulster or some type of re-partition arrangement. A united Ireland is an obvious alternative scenario to consider, and our concern here is purely to examine the economic implications of such an option. The basic conclusion is that though some significant improvement could result, many of the underlying problems would remain. That leads us to consider a more radical option, which would entail significant social and political transformation to achieve a democratically accountable economy. Though this chapter is to some extent speculative, it does seek a realistic evaluation of the economic implications of various political options. What it does not do, however, is consider fully the political viability of the various economic scenarios. It simply provides some of the tools and the basic analysis for political debate which seeks a way out of the present impasse.

1

Dependent Development

Every country seeks to achieve the maximum possible level of economic development. Orthodox economic development theories stress the benefits of integration within the capitalist world economy. This model assumes that each country will benefit through specialization and the free play of market forces. The theory is that this will lead to a harmonious unfolding of productive forces, to be followed by a modernization of society as a whole. In short everything will be for the best in this best of all possible worlds. The historical record, however, shows that there are winners and losers in the international economic development game. There is not much point in comparing Ireland and India, for example, with Britain if the latter was, for a whole era, the colonial power which explicitly prevented economic development in what was then part of the British Empire. Another way of putting it, is that not all the countries in the globe are travelling on the same railway line with the same inexorable destiny of economic development. In a world of huge economic, political, military and strategic inequalities this is not a realistic model. There is really not much to recommend orthodox modernization theory as a means of understanding the development of the Irish economy. Most Irish economic historians, even those of the 'revisionist' school which opposes what it sees as the myths of nationalist history, are too aware of the historical context of the Irish experience to fall into this trap.

Another approach to Irish development or, rather, underdevelopment derives from the tradition of Irish nationalism. From the orthodox tendency to ignore the international context, the nationalist reading of economic history focuses almost exclusively on the role of Britain. The danger here is that Britain and British economic policies become the source of all Ireland's economic ills, when in fact the historical record is usually rather more complicated. It was actually specific social interests in Britain which benefited from the economic exploitations of

1

Ireland. It was British capitalism and not 'perfidious Albion' which caused Irish underdevelopment. The other side of the coin is that it is not a nation as such which is exploited but, again, specific social classes. The nationalist approach tends to ride roughshod over social differentiation and social conflict within Ireland. Between the ahistorical orthodox approach and the asocial nationalist approach to Irish economic development there is not much to choose from.

It is not our intention to steer an impossible middle course between these two interpretations. Rather we pursue an alternative which seeks to avoid the pitfalls of both. 'Dependent development' expresses in a nutshell the view of Irish history proposed: that development has occurred (contrary to some versions of the nationalist thesis) but that it has been dependent (against the harmonious view of the orthodox development theories).

Dependency has been defined as a 'conditioning situation' in which the dominant economies set the terms on which others may develop. A situation of dependence causes these latter countries to be both backward and exploited. In some popular versions of this approach it was argued that the greater the level of contact with the advanced countries, the greater the level of underdevelopment ('development of underdevelopment' was the catchphrase). In fact, the Latin American originators of the dependency approach always recognized that dependency and development were not incompatible (in other words 'dependent development'). What makes the approach still relevant today is its nuanced methodology which avoids the problems of both orthodox modernization theory and economic nationalism. In brief, this inter-disciplinary approach combines the insight of economics, politics and sociology. It is, above all, both structural and historical, stressing as it does not only the structural conditioning of society, but also the historical transformation of these societies through social conflict. Finally, against popularized versions, the Latin American dependency authors did not emphasize exclusively the external aspect of dependency (imperialism in short) but recognized the complex interaction between external conditioning and the internal social and political struggles of a nation.

Although rejecting any false dichotomy between 'external' and 'internal' aspects of dependency, we may start by listing some of the first. The main external factor causing dependency is the domination by foreign interests over the key sectors of the economy. If foreign ownership and control over the most dynamic economic sectors is the main form of dependency it can, however, be manifested in other more indirect forms. These may include technological dependence (patents, know-how, etc.), financial dependence (through the IMF or the World Bank for example) and trade dependence. This last may take different forms, from trade patterns inherited from the colonial era to the general 'unequal exchange' which occurs between agrarian and industrial goods due to the deteriorating terms of trade. Unequal exchange transfers part of the economic surplus generated in the dependent economies to the dominant economies, thus diminishing the chances of successful development. The most noticeable recent form of external dependence is the huge foreign debt accumulated in some countries, the repayment of which, at onerous interest rates, is crippling their development prospects. It is important to stress, finally, that the 'external' aspects of dependence are always internalized, thus creating structurally deficient and unbalanced social and economic structures.

The main internal aspect of dependency is the uneven nature of development which causes widespread poverty, unemployment and, often, mass migration. This set of issues is sometimes subsumed under the term 'structural heterogeneity' as caused by the uneven distribution of the fruits of technical progress. The disparities in productivity caused by foreign investment lead to inter-sectoral imbalances, a widening of income differentials and a growing marginalization of the population outside the dynamic sector. The local dominant class (or 'dependent bourgeoisie') is increasingly incapable, under these conditions, of creating an autonomous capitalist path of development. The development which does take place is thus in association with the dominant economies, in particular the transnational corporations. The links of dependence are thus strengthened while, at the same time, the state tends to exclude growing sections of society from participation in the benefits of development. The dependent nation state is thus not sovereign in either economic or political terms, a state of affairs dictated equally by internal forces as much as by external ones. Without overcoming dependency, underdevelopment will persist, as will economic subordination and, thus, emancipation be it economic, political, social or cultural will be frustrated.

If we are to examine the Irish economy from a dependency perspective we should, even at this early stage, ask whether a *non*-dependent development model is actually feasible. At first dependency writers operated with a basic unwritten assumption that socialist revolution (the 'Cuban path') was the simple and obvious way to overcome dependence. However, the case of Cuba itself shows how difficult it is to diversify an ex-colonial economy and achieve a degree of self-reliance. The example of Cambodia show how politically disastrous the extreme recipe of autarchy (withdrawal from the world economy) to cure dependency was. The concept of 'delinking' was developed to overcome the obvious problems of autarchy. It assumes a more limited (sectoral and temporal) disengagement from external commercial, financial and technological exchanges. It implies the choice of economic options on a national basis and with popular relevance, breaking this from the criteria of pure economic nationality operating on a world scale. Through delinking the dependent country could, according to this perspective, begin to construct a more balanced economy and to overcome the legacies of colonialism and dependence.

Dependency reversal also needs to take place with regard to the internal facets such as structural heterogeneity referred to above. This would be an 'autocentric' model of development, capable of meeting the material needs of the whole population as its main priority. This type of development would be self-sustained (that is not dependent) and sustainable (that is, ecologically sound) in the long term. Delinking on its own might create the conditions for 'dependency reversal' but its success depends ultimately on the profound internal structural reforms necessary to overcome the obstacles to domestic market expansion and productive, dynamic development. This, in turn, creates the conditions to overcome poverty, structural unemployment, emigration and famine.

Having presented a brief synopsis of our theoretical framework we pass now to our broad sweep of 'dependent development' in Ireland.

Early developments

Celtic Ireland possessed an economy where grass and cattle prevailed over crop growing. The society which went along with this economic system can be characterized as tribal pastoralism. As Raymond Crotty points out: 'The cold, wet climate and the related woodland clearances militated against the emergence of the sort of capital-based crop-growing that evolved in Central Western Europe.'[1] The Norman Conquest of the eleventh and twelfth centuries turned the economy more towards crop growing and laid the basis for the feudal system which eventually replaced Gaelic society. The Norman lords carved out a small domain for themselves where crop and pasture land coexisted under the wing of the feudal castle. Yet settling the forest wildernesses of Ireland was not always crowned by success. Not for nothing had the Romans dismissed Ireland as not worthy of invasion. In the event, by the fourteenth century the Normans had been largely forced back to the safe, dry and somewhat warmer southeast of Ireland known as the Pale. It was not a great Gaelic revival which led to the re-emergence of tribal pastoralism but, on the whole, the unfavourable economic conditions. Nevertheless, Ireland was proving easier to conquer than to hold for outside powers.

It was Henry VII, the Tudor King of England, who in the fifteenth century declared himself King of Ireland and thus began a new era of conquest. Whereas hitherto England's rule over Ireland had been largely nominal, there now began a concerted move towards real as against formal subjection of the Irish economy. It was not the salvation of souls which concerned the new invaders nor even the seeking of precious metals. In Ireland there was a strategic motive for colonization – protecting England's western flank from rival maritime powers – but above all, the compulsion to acquire Irish land. In 1601 the Battle of Kinsale opened the way for the Elizabethan conquest and the appropriation of the Irish clan lands as English private property. Around this time the Irish economy was relatively undeveloped, with exports being restricted to fish and hides. Yet during the first half of the seventeenth century there was a significant modernization of Irish agriculture. Cattle exports grew as did those of wool and butter. By 1870 there was even 1,000 tons of iron ore being produced annually. As L.M. Cullen in his broad survey of the Irish economy notes, 'From a woodland society Ireland was emerging as an agricultural region with a substantial agricultural surplus.'[2]

The Irish economy did not, however, enter a period of steady, undisturbed growth with gradual diversification and an essential natural industrialization. Instead, Ireland was to be ravaged by war in the seventeenth century. Between 1641 and 1652 war brought plague and famine to Ireland, crops failed, cattle were destroyed and over half a million people died. The defeat of the final act of resistance by the Gaelic clan chiefs led to a wholesale confiscation of Irish lands. Whereas Catholics still owned 60 per cent of the land in 1640, this proportion had fallen to 14 per cent by 1690. Oliver Cromwell's soldiers and the financiers of the English armies were all awarded land, but Irish tenants still usually stayed on under the new English landlords. Only in Ulster was a genuine settler capitalism to take root as a response to the resistance of the native Irish. For a time the export of cattle and sheep, particularly in the transatlantic trade, prospered but renewed war between 1689 and 1697 again depleted the supply of livestock through plunder, destruction or military acquisition. Belfast and the northeast prospered in the aftermath of the Williamite wars, but overall the history of war and its consequent inevitable economic dislocation prevented the organic development of the Irish economy in this period.

England was now entering a period of mercantilism which preceded capitalism and was based on the country's strong navy and the exploitation through trade of other economies, such as the Irish one. For mercantilism to be effective as a replacement for direct plunder, it was necessary to restrict production in the periphery, for example, Ireland. Thus the Cattle Acts of 1663 placed prohibitive duties on cattle or sheep exported from Ireland, these duties being extended in 1667 to beef and pork. The crucial Navigation Acts of 1663 forced all goods destined for the colonies to be shipped from England leading, for example, to the decline of Galway. In 1669 the export of woollen goods from Ireland was also prohibited, with subsequent Acts being directed against brewing and glass manufacturing. Some economic historians have questioned whether these measures were in the interests of the British state or were taken merely to protect certain specific vested economic interest there. There is also debate on the precise impact of the various Acts, with other factors such as bad crops being identified. Essentially, however, each measure individually and especially as a package was instrumental in making the Irish economy dependent on Britain and in thwarting the possibility of balanced economic growth.

The balance-sheet of economic development in Ireland during the seventeenth century is not a simple one. For contemporaries such as Jonathan Swift, the 1699 Act regarding wool destroyed the Irish woollen industry, led to widespread migration of weavers and caused a general economic decline. Yet economic historians such as Cullen insist that 'English policy was not, however, inimical in intent towards Ireland . . . there was no intention to restrain Irish foreign trade or the country's economic development.'[3] Perhaps we are dealing then with the unintended consequences of actions. A picture of unrelieved gloom would certainly not be justified. The 1680s, for example, saw the beginning of a long and sustained growth of linen exports from Ireland: from 23,000 yards in 1683 to 520,000 in 1705. A population of around two and a half million at the turn of the century was also not a reflection of stagnation. The reality is that development took place but it was dependent development. Sir William Petty in his *Treatise of Ireland* of 1687 exemplified, in an extreme way perhaps, how British capitalism viewed Ireland: he proposed that the people of Ireland should be largely removed to provide labourers in England and the country could then be converted into a huge cattlewalk to feed Britain. Profit was here associated with a radical solution to the 'Irish question'.

In the northeast province of Ulster a rather different approach to the problem was put into practice. Gaelic Ulster had been one of the strongest bastions against the Normans and resisted the Tudor conquest most stubbornly. In the seventeenth century there were, at the same time, considerable numbers of Scottish and English farmers being driven off the land by sheep farming. So, the colonization of Ulster by these mainly Protestant settlers became an attractive option. The Plantation of Ulster, unique in Europe and with only few parallels in African colonialism, would, as Crotty argues, 'make more secure the metropolis's control over the whole island'.[4] It certainly did this but also sowed the seeds for the partition of Ireland and the growing intractability of the 'Irish question'. In terms of economic development Belfast was being described in 1688 by a contemporary as 'the second town of Ireland, well built, full of people, and of great trade'. This was certainly an exaggeration, but by the end of the century Belfast had become the fourth most important port in the country. The once backward northeast of Ireland was also well placed to participate in the forthcoming British Industrial Revolution as part of the Belfast, Liverpool, Glasgow triangle.

Land, industry and growth

The general trend of the Irish economy in the eighteenth century was one of sustained expansion and growth. This was the period of proto-industrialization or industrialization before the Industrial Revolution itself occurred. In this phase factory industry established itself outside towns, in country areas where water-power provided the main source of power. From 1770 onwards Britain's famous Industrial Revolution began to have a huge effect in Ireland, on industry, transport, banking and the social and economic life of the country as a whole. However, all was not rosy in the eighteenth century. Development took place within a context of increased dependency. A simple but effective index of this dependency was the increase in the proportion of Irish exports heading to Britain from 44 per cent of the total in 1720 to 85 per cent in 1800. Britain's role in Ireland's export trade thus nearly doubled during the century. Furthermore, rent from Irish land increased from £800,000 in 1670 to £8 million in 1800, a massive tenfold increase in rent revenue. The eighteenth century was also a period of regular bank and credit failures, as well as the regular sequence of crop failures and famines. Irish development was not only dependent, but also extremely cyclical.

The clear-cut success story of the eighteenth century was undoubtedly the linen industry. Unlike the treatment of the woollen industry, flax and linen production was encouraged by the British government with an Act of 1696 allowing Irish linens to be imported duty free. British settlers and the Huguenots (French Protestant refugees) of the northeast were to play a dominant role in this centralized trade. A measure of its dynamism is the increase in linen exports from Ireland, from half a million yards at the start of the century to over 40 million yards per annum towards the end of the eighteenth century. Ulster accounted for approximately 80 per cent of these exports. Though Ulster dominated the linen industry, a rural textile industry was expanding throughout Ireland in the crucial period leading up to the Industrial Revolution. The depression of 1773 however, seriously threatened the industry with up to two-thirds of the looms in the country lying idle. In Ulster the recovery from this blow was swifter than in other parts of Ireland to some extent because the weavers had retained their small plots of land which they could fall back on. By 1782 Belfast was able to challenge the role of Dublin as the clearing-house for Irish linens and was becoming the main link to the British market.

Other important textile sectors were the cotton and woollen industries. The exclusion of Irish woollen imports from Britain in 1699 was, as O'Malley notes, 'in itself an indication of the contemporary English evaluation of the competitive potential of early Irish industry'.[5] Though barred from the English market the industry continued to provide for the home market. It was the cotton industry, however, which was to prove most dynamic in its effects. It was the cotton industry which, in the 1780s, was to first deploy the mechanized technology of the Industrial Revolution in Ireland. Belfast was to be the major location of the industry, with over half of the country's spinning capacity, vital insofar as this was the most mechanized stage of cotton production. The Irish parliament vigorously supported the cotton industry, through grants to firms, bounties on home sales and exports and a substantial tariff on imports which, surprisingly, included British goods. However, the economies of scale and Ireland's dependent position with regard to the British economy would eventually take their toll. In the 1780s the Irish cotton industry was comparable in terms of size to that of Scotland but by the turn of the century, due to slow growth, it was only about a quarter of its size. Imitation of another country's pattern of industrialization was to prove a most uncertain road to development.

Textiles were not the only thriving branch of industry. There were large mechanized firms involved in flour milling, for example, by the 1760s which, in fact, set the pattern for the early cotton-spinning mills. They used what was then the novel method of the manufacturer also being active in the marketing of the product. As Cullen points out, 'These flour millers represented a new pattern of economic organisation.'[6] Production methods also developed, with the weavers, for example, ceasing to be independent craftworkers and, instead, becoming dependent on the work 'put out' to them by the bleachers. Capital was becoming a major factor of production with the profits of landowners and merchants often being invested in industry. But capitalism meant more than just capital, because it began to transform the very structure of society and the relations of production on which it was based. Though industry on the scale of Yorkshire did not emerge, some factory-type firms were set up in the last quarter of the eighteenth century. There was a strong tendency towards centralization in this industry, with its location influenced strongly by the availability of skilled labour.

The idea of proto-industrialization seems to account quite well for the developments which began in the mid eighteenth century. As Liam Kennedy explains, proto-industrialization 'refers to peasant handicrafts production, where commodities are destined for markets beyond the local and regional context, and where there is a symbiotic relationship between rural industry and commercial agriculture'.[7] This proto-industrialization was characteristic of the linen industry, particularly in the northeast. It promoted the accumulation of capital, and both the labour skills and technical expertise necessary to achieve the full transition to capitalism. This transition did not, of course, always materialize and some regions slipped back to a dependence on agriculture. The aspect referring to export orientation was certainly the case in Ulster. The rural economy thus contributed to industrialization through proto-industrialization, but it is well to recall that the prosperity of one area was usually built on the decline of the other. In general, following Liam Kennedy, we must recall that 'there was no automatic take-off from the sites of proto-industrial activity into the clear skies of self-sustaining growth'.[8]

In the domain of agriculture itself the potato now became supreme. It allowed profits to be derived from Irish lands after the Cattle Acts prevented the export of livestock to Britain. It also provided sufficient sustenance to reproduce the labour force with minimal investment. As Crotty explains, 'The exotic potato thus created in Ireland the agronomic conditions in which a coolie class could subsist by cultivating land without capital, other than a spade and a basket of seed potatoes.'[9] This development occurred most rapidly during the second half of the eighteenth century, providing a ready pool of labour for Ireland's but, above all, Britain's industries. The fortunes of the rest of agriculture were tied closely to market conditions, particularly in the case of grain, where farms were much smaller than in grazing districts. Periodic famines were the inevitable result. The lack of security of tenure for the tenant was a particularly live issue. Not surprisingly, by the turn of the century there were several active agrarian secret societies in various parts of the country. We should not forget that Ireland was still a predominantly rural society and that the economic and social upheavals of the countryside were to play a major role in the political arena.

The northeast of Ireland was now indisputably becoming the most dynamic area of the economy. The symbiotic relationship between rural industry and commercial agriculture referred to above was a crucial factor here. It is often said that Ulster became the main locale of the linen industry because in other provinces the rack renting of tenants prevented this emergence of petty commodity producers. However, most economic historians have found that the linen industry spread widely in spite of different land tenure systems. The spinning part of the industry actually grew faster outside Ulster. In the cotton industry too, although Belfast became the main cotton-spinning locale, Dublin was a far larger regional centre overall. There were, of course, advantages in the northeast for the early stages of industrialization such as the ready supply of skilled labour in the Lagan Valley area. The settlers of the northeast attracted capital and specific groups, like the Huguenots, provided essential technical inputs. But the overall explanation of the northeast's greater level of industrialization lies in a cumulative causation involving a number of these factors. As Kieran Kennedy writes:

Whatever initial advantages the Belfast area possessed in the way of a more settled agricultural system, a more extensive domestic textile industry, and a key trading centre were greatly magnified over time as industrial skills were acquired, venture capital accumulated and success in one activity opened up other possibilities.[10]

This virtuous cycle of development once set in motion was to reinforce itself ever more strongly. This does not mean, however, that life was rosy for the early textile workers, for example. Certainly data for the early nineteenth century shows a per capita income for Ulster slightly below the national average, and we find that both poverty intensified and inequalities increased in this period.

This was also a century in which economic nationalism became increasingly popular in Ireland, especially during the period of Grattan's parliament from 1782 to 1801. The members of this parliament shared the era's dominant ideas on the 'rights of man' or, more specifically, the rights of the property-owning classes. With England preoccupied by the American War of Independence it secured in 1782 the abolition of the 1494 Poyning's Law which had prevented the Irish parliament from meeting without royal licence. British restrictions on trade, particularly that on wool, hit hardest at the manufacturers and traders, and it was this sector which agitated for protectionist measures through Grattan's parliament. This period has been mythologized in nationalist historiography, with Sinn Fein founder Arthur Griffith declaring that:

> Grattan's Parliament was able to revive and stimulate Irish trade and commerce to a degree of prosperity which it had not enjoyed for centuries ... [It] turned Ireland into a large exporter of manufactured goods ... and secured recognition in every part of Europe for the mercantile flag of Ireland.[11]

The socialist James Connolly was far less sanguine, denying that legislative independence in itself could fundamentally alter the workings of the underlying economic process. This view accords with the analysis of economic historians like Cullen for whom 'the industrial development of the period owed little to legislative measures or to financial assistance of the legislature'.[12] Certainly, the economic advances had begun in mid century long before Grattan's parliament whose policies were, in a sense, nothing new. Yet there is still an important lesson to be learned from this period. State support for industrialization is a necessary if not sufficient element for its success. An element of protectionism is also essential for countries which enter late into the development process. But all of this was to change with the Act of Union which terminated this early move towards Irish independence.

The eighteenth century, viewed from a long-term perspective, was one of relative economic advancement in Ireland. This was reflected in an increase of the total population to approximately 5 million by the end of the century. There was even the emergence of a substantial Catholic middle class, who succeeded to some extent in overcoming the detrimental effects of the various 'anti-popery' laws. We can also note a significant increase in the importation of luxury goods such as tea, tobacco and sugar into the country. Yet all of these developments were set in the context of continuing dependency. As Crotty has remarked, profits generated in Ireland were 'in contrast to the profits from English landed property, used for the most part in ways that reduced rather than increase Irish national product'.[13] Profit from the land was partly invested in cattle or sheep, which, if more profitable, still tended to reduce agricultural output. But, most significantly, the rest of the profits were simply transferred to London as rent to absentee landowners. Ironically these funds, and the savings of small farmers, thus contributed to Britain's Industrial Revolution which in turn contributed to the decline of craft and cottage industries in Ireland.

Nineteenth-century decline

If the dominant tone of the eighteenth century was one of expansion, in the nineteenth century there was a dramatic decline in Ireland's economic fortune. The exodus from agriculture accelerated, with a declining industrial base unable to take up the surplus labour. The mid-century famine breaks up the period into pre- and post-famine times. The century begins, however, with the Act of Union which was a response to the great political upheavals of 1798 and the failure of the United Irishmen's rising. Britain's Prime Minister Pitt had declared in its aftermath that 'The Union is the only answer to preventing Ireland becoming too great and powerful.' If the causes of the Act of Union were largely political and strategic, its effects on the economy would be profound. Henceforth, repeal of the Act of Union would be the key demand of all nationalist movements. The Act also signifies a new mode of regulation of the Irish economy as industrial capitalism had by this stage begun to consolidate its grip over the British social and economic structure. The Irish economy now assumed the dependent position of classical imperialism whereby it was subordinated as a provider of cheap labour and raw materials to the dominant power. It is a crucial period to study in relation to current economic debates between free traders and a more nationalist course.

The end of legislative independence for Ireland did not lead immediately to full economic union with Britain. A compromise was reached in relation to those Irish industries, mainly luxury consumer goods, which had hitherto enjoyed tariff protection. Protection of Irish woollen manufactures was also conceded until 1820. In practice, the Irish economy remained relatively buoyant until the end of the Napoleonic Wars in 1815, but did not recover from the postwar recession in 1820 as other areas did. Britain was now at the height of the Industrial Revolution and as E.R. Green, amongst others, has noted, 'Industrial undertakings in less favoured regions such as Ireland became uncompetitive and sooner or later went to the wall.'[14] British industry, having had the benefits of protectionism while it suited, now preached the virtues of free trade and open competition. Yet this was a somewhat unequal competition with Irish industry being quite unable to compete on equal terms with the 'workshop of the world' that Britain had become. With over three-quarters of Irish trade being with Britain, the Irish economy would also suffer from the crises of British capitalism such as that of 1826 and, later, in the 1870s.

The picture of nineteenth century economic decline in Ireland is a dramatic one. The crisis was most marked in the linen industry at first with other sectors such as milling, brewing and shipbuilding continuing to expand even though they were becoming more centralized. The decline was also spread unevenly in spatial terms. Thus, while Belfast expanded as an industrial centre (on which, more later), areas such as Cork suffered. One town, Bandon, had over 1,500 weavers in 1830 and ten years later, in 1840, only 150 weavers remained in business. Drogheda, once a major textile centre, saw the number of handloom weavers drop by three-quarters over the same period. The woollen and cotton industries also contracted severely during the first half of the nineteenth century. A long-term view of the textile industry graphically illustrates the nineteenth-century decline: in 1841 the industry employed 700,000 people, one-fifth of the working population, but at the turn of the century there were only 92,000 textile workers in Ireland. The inevitable sequel of industrial decline and economic failure was the decline in the workforce from 3.5 million in 1840 to 1.8 million in 1910. Of course, the Great Famine was to greatly accentuate this demographic collapse.

The Great Famine which began in 1845 is still considered a significant watershed in Irish economic history, even if more recent research sees it as accentuating pre-existing trends and not the abrupt break it was previously considered. The Famine began as a result of a failure of the potato crop, a blight which returned in four successive years. Between 1845 and 1850, the population fell by about 2 million, 1 million died and 1 million emigrated. Some economists point out that fever claimed more victims than starvation but such a fine distinction seems irrelevant: certainly as the Famine-hit labourers and small holders of the west and south migrated north and east they brought fever with them. There is also the point that government intervention might have been counter-productive because it 'could have harmed the fragile but extensive retail system that catered for food requirements in much of the country'.[15] The fact remains that government intervention to alleviate the effects of the famine were delayed and made ineffective by a doctrinaire clinging to the tenets of laissez-faire or non-intervention central to free trade economics. There is the further argument, of course, that it was the British land policy in Ireland which created the conditions for the Famine in the first place.

The roots of the Famine lay not in some Malthusian 'excess of population' but, rather, in the system of land tenure which condemned the vast majority of the population to under- and unemployment. Its effects were a dramatic concentration in landholdings, with the number of farms of less than 5 acres falling by nearly three-quarters between 1841 and 1851. As Marx noted in 1861 the effects of this were 'positive' from a capitalist logic, because 'the Irish famine of 1846 killed more than 1,000,000 people, but it killed poor devils only. To the wealth of the country it did not the slightest damage.'[16] The Famine had the effect of accelerating and consolidating a virtual revolution in land-tenure. It had three main results: the decline of the population by one-third between 1840 and 1880, the doubling of the average size of landholdings, and the shift towards pasture farming (livestock) and away from tillage as a result of market forces. Capitalism was now consolidating its grip on Irish agriculture, a process to be completed with the Land Acts of 1881 and 1903 (see Chapter 4 for more detail).

Post-Famine Ireland was not characterized by a total economic collapse. The urban populations remained steady, and those of Dublin and Belfast rose sharply. Industry, according to most economic historians, remained prosperous in the 1850s and 1860s. There were some notable success stories such as the Guinness brewery in Dublin which ended the century as the biggest brewery in the world. Yet by the 1870s Irish industry was in crisis and the 1880s have been described by Cullen as 'a grim decade'.[17] The steamroller of British industrial production was simply overwhelming craft production in Ireland. For example, factory-produced iron-goods made the blacksmith obsolete. The advent of the sewing machine led to a two-thirds reduction in the number of bootmakers between 1870 and the turn of the century. On top of this structural decline came the end of the international capitalist boom in 1874, after which, as Cullen recounts, 'British manufacturers flooded the Irish market and prices fell.'[18] The industrial crisis coincided with one in agriculture making its effect even more severe. But the decline was now deep-rooted enough that even good harvests would not reverse it.

The decline of the cotton industry after the Act of Union led paradoxically to the revival of the linen industry in the northeast and particularly around the Belfast area. Between 1830 and the Famine the population of Belfast, now heavily dependent on linen, practically doubled. At first it was only spinning which was carried out mechanically, but after the Famine power-loom weaving was introduced. The American Civil War in the 1860s had the fortuitous effect (for Ireland) of reducing the cotton supplies and thus increasing the demand for linen. By now Ulster had become the largest linen-producing area in the world. The expanding textile industries encouraged the development of complementary branches of engineering such as steam engine construction. The specialized craft of boiler-making was especially important, not only in its own right but because of its subsequent links with shipbuilding. Other specialist firms included Davidson and Co which pioneered the production of tea-drying equipment in the 1880s and was to go on to supply three-quarters of the world's requirements. All these developments taken together amount to a veritable industrial revolution. The leap forward of industrialization in the northeast is graphically illustrated by the dramatic increase in the population of Belfast, from around 20,000 people at the start of the nineteenth century to some 400,000 by its close.

The other major new industry developed in the northeast was, of course, shipbuilding with the area accounting for one-quarter of UK tonnage being built by the end of the century. The building of iron ships was not a simple extension of wooden ones and the new technology developed in Belfast thus eclipsed the rest of Irish shipbuilding. After some less than auspicious attempts the firm of Harland and Wolff began to build ships in the second half of the 1850s. They were joined by a smaller yard in 1879 and Belfast soon had the second and the fourth largest shipbuilders in the UK. This success should not, however, be interpreted as full and equal participation in the Industrial Revolution. The experience of iron-founding is significant in this regard because Belfast firms were affected as much as those in the rest of Ireland by British competition. As O'Malley points out:

> similar remarks about the failure of particular engineering industries in the north east, due to the absence of a sufficiently large local market and the existence of specialised producers elsewhere, apply to locomotives and most machine tools, as well as the new generation of consumer durables.[19]

The other 'downside' to what seemed an economic miracle could be the almost total dependence on trade with Britain and the British Empire.

For an overview of this whole period we can refer to Michael Hechter who has analyzed Ireland's position in terms of 'internal colonialism': 'On the eve of the Act of Union the development prospects of the Irish economy appeared very favourable ... After the Union, Ireland became more rural, more agricultural, more economically specialized than it had been previously.'[20] Certainly, this view to some extent neglects the industrialization drive of the northeast but as an overall view it is incontestable. It is not surprising in this context that one eminent contemporary critic, Karl Marx, could write in the 1860s that what Ireland needed was '1. Self-government and independence from England. 2. An agrarian revolution. 3. Protective tariffs against England.'[21] Later Marx observed that 'every time Ireland was about to develop industrially, she was crushed and reconverted into a purely agricultural land'.[22] This analysis is significant because it predates the development of a theory of imperialism (let alone a dependency theory) and it contrasts with Marx's generally favourable view of free trade and of the prospects of capitalism spreading to all parts of the globe.

It is the causes of this industrial decline in the nineteenth century which we must now examine. One view is that Ireland quite simply lacked the prerequisites for an industrial revolution in terms of natural and human resources. The lack of coal and iron in Ireland is often suggested as a drawback. Yet this cannot be an absolute block on industrialization, especially when we consider that there was no scarcity of capital in Ireland, the rail network was well developed and there was a plentiful supply of educated labour power. Another suggestion is that Ireland's capitalist class lacked that mysterious ingredient for success known as entrepreneurship. Joseph Lee has advance this line of argument pointing to the role of immigrant businessmen such as Harland (of Harland and Wolff). Yet all this example shows is that there were profitable areas for investment in the northeast, not that a more competent local capital class could have created more development. In fact, Irish capitalists were able to reorganize the non-textile sectors of industry quite well in the nineteenth century. Nor was British and other overseas investment that extensive in Ireland, focusing on particular profitable openings, suggesting as O'Malley notes that 'profitable opportunities for wider industrialization were not particularly evident to them either'.[23] It would seem that other causes should be investigated.

In nationalist commentaries on this period major emphasis is placed on the lack of protective tariffs after the Act of Union and British hostility to a strong independent Ireland. British rule per se cannot be seen as intrinsically hostile to development in Ireland because at times development (albeit dependent) did occur. Nor was the withdrawal of tariffs the sole cause of industrial decline in the nineteenth century. Essentially, the nationalist focus on tariffs is too narrow and we need to examine the whole social and economic structure of dependency. Essentially, the development of capitalism in Britain created massive centralizing tendencies which led to a 'rationalization' of economies it interacted with. The growing advantages of large-scale firms also had a damaging effect in Ireland. Crotty points to the decline of the Irish market as a result of changes in agriculture. Brian Girvin in an overview has argued that the 'objective obstacles to development' in Ireland 'may be external but are more likely to be internal'.[24] It would seem from our analysis, however, that there can be no hard and fast distinction between internal and external factors like this. Indeed, the internal socioeconomic transformations cannot be divorced from the apparently 'external' operations of imperialism.

Eoin O'Malley argues that the Irish experience during this period 'conflicts with the view that the attainment of favourable local conditions and reliance on free market forces is sufficient to generate industrial development'.[25] Indeed, before the Industrial Revolution, Irish industry had become a considerable force and certainly conditions for industrialization were not particularly adverse. As to free market

forces, the effects were almost totally disastrous, although protectionism may not have been a panacea. The free operation of market forces
meant death or emigration for a whole layer of the population and
effectively blocked the development of a balanced, integrated and
dynamic national economy. The favoured status of the northeast with
its partial integration into Britain's developing industrial economy
cannot change this overall conclusion. Not only did it create the basis
for the politically disastrous partition of the country but also was itself
largely based on the decline of other areas, even within the north, which
were drawn under by Belfast's industrial expansion.

Towards independence

As we move into the twentieth century, economic debate is largely
subsumed by dramatic political events. It is essential, however, to carry
out a systematic balance-sheet of the state of economy on the eve of
independence and, of course, partition in 1920. It is a mixed and even
uncertain balance-sheet we are dealing with. Agriculture had a run of
unprecedented boom years during the First World War, but this was
followed by a slump after 1920. There were demands made by some for
nationalist-inspired protection of local industries, yet others (in the
north) strove for closer integration with Britain. We even have
disagreement on the overall tenor of the Irish development experience
as a whole. For many the issue in 1920 was why had Ireland not
industrialized? Yet respected economic historian L.M. Cullen states
categorically that 'Ireland was in many respects a highly developed
country by the end of the [nineteenth] century.'[26] This was also a country
of high emigration rates but where the standard of living at home was
quite respectable in comparative terms, according to the latest calcula-
tions. It is this picture of uneven development which we will seek to
clarify in this final section. It is the necessary background to the
subsequent studies of the Republic's economy (Chapter 2) and that of
Northern Ireland (Chapter 3).

The northeast epitomizes this picture of uneven development. On the
one hand, the population of Belfast doubled between 1880 and 1900,
but for the rest of Ulster, on the other hand, the picture was less positive.
Cullen writes of the linen industry that 'behind the facade of this
spectacular process of centralisation around Belfast, the industry does
not represent a reassuring picture of prosperity'.[27] Derry in the

northwest perhaps best exemplifies the precarious nature of the north's industrialization. The 5 shirt-making factories of the 1850s had become 38 by the early twentieth century. This provided low-wage female employment in the city, but also depended on rural women with extremely poor wages for home work carrying out the sewing end of the process. Thus the wages of this industry could not even support a family let alone generate a cycle of consumption and development. Cullen points out quite accurately that: 'Derry was, despite its rapid growth [its population doubled between 1850 and 1900], a poor city, and the origins of its twentieth-century economic problems can be detected in the fragile character of its nineteenth-century prosperity.'[28] Dependency on one product could, ultimately, prove as debilitating as dependency on another economy.

In the rest of the country industrialization was even more uneven. On the one hand, Irish whiskey, Dublin's porter (Guinness) and biscuits (Jacobs), alongside Belfast's linen and ships had an international reputation. It is estimated that around half of the country's agricultural and industrial output was exported. Today, that would be considered a success story for export-led development strategies. On the other hand, a more detailed examination of the Irish economy shows a far less reassuring picture. In 1911 around 35 per cent of the labour force in the northeast was engaged in industry, but for the rest of the country the proportion was only 13 per cent. Ireland was still an overwhelmingly rural economy and industry was highly concentrated around just one city, Belfast. The thriving export-oriented sectors of foodprocessing or drink in the south accounted for around two-thirds of manufacturing output. Again, the concentration of industry in a few sectors or regions reinforced the highly uneven development of the economy. Elsewhere, the pattern was one of deindustrialization and a continuation, albeit somewhat slower, of emigration, a sure sign of an economy lacking dynamism and prospects.

In agriculture the first decades of the twentieth century show a markedly uneven pattern. On the one hand, between 1910 and 1920 agricultural prices nearly trebled. Favourable terms of trade led to increased prosperity for the already prosperous banks and a general improvement for the farming community. Though wages as usual lagged behind rising prices, emigration sharply decreased in this period. However, by 1920 the boom was over as prices began to drop again. As Cullen writes:

Economic dislocation was considerable. Businessmen or farmers who had borrowed money were in great difficulties; the banks themselves were gravely embarrassed by the fall in the value of shares or land pledged as a collateral for loans; and unemployment increased.[29]

Of course, during this period life in the country was dominated by political upheavals. Rural labourers and smallholders joined the fight for national independence through the Irish Republican Army and/or engaged in fierce class struggle in their own right. Then the civil war between 1922 and 1923 tore the country apart in events which quite overshadowed the economic contraction of the period.

The politics of development during this period became polarized around the nationalist and pro-British Unionist positions respectively. A conscious political support for Irish industry had already emerged in the last decades of the nineteenth century. Arthur Griffith of Sinn Fein was prominent in advancing the case for an Irish industry protected by tariff barriers. In 1905, the Irish Industrial Development Association was formed which not only sought to promote public awareness of Irish industry and products, but also secured a legally recognized market for Irish goods. Though traders themselves were mainly sceptical of the benefits of tariffs – sharing the dominant British free-trade outlook – the issue of protectionism gradually came to the fore in the early twentieth century. Cullen writes that this movement 'tended to overestimate Ireland's natural advantages and resources, and hence, as a rule, assumed optimistically that under altered political arrangements much of the country's industrial recovery would be spontaneous'.[30] Undoubtedly this naive expectation was unrealistic and the focus on tariffs was excessively narrow. Nevertheless, this movement was correct in its implicit conclusion that favourable natural conditions together with free trade were not sufficient to promote economic development in Ireland.

In the northeast, the dominant industrial and commercial interests would, understandably, have little sympathy with these nationalist aspirations. As one northern newspaper noted at the turn on the century, 'our commercial and manufacturing classes are devoted to the Union because they know that trade and commerce would not flourish without the Union'. On this basis, the northern capitalists threw their weight behind the Unionist cause, which had gradually become a specifically Ulster rather than Irish Unionism. Protestant workers also tended to be

Unionist from the point of view of economic self-interest insofar as the union of Ulster (or eventually part of the province) with the British economy would ensure a continuation of investment, guaranteed markets and, consequently, jobs. In this scenario, as Gibbon explains, 'Home Rule signalled not only economic disaster but also the interruption of the extension of social reforms to the working class, reforms "guaranteed" by the participation of Ireland in the empire.'[31] In the event, the years between the two World Wars would be ones of depression and unemployment for the northern economy. The advantages to labour of the reforms which industry felt compelled to grant to its 'loyal' workers were by no means illusory but were still severely limited.

On the eve of partition there were two distinct modes of production in Ireland. One, in the north, was centred around machine-minding industry and skilled crafts, and the other, in the south, centred around small-scale farming, with only a limited industrial sector. An analysis based on the notions of uneven and dependent development cannot simply repeat the nationalist interpretation. There was nothing 'unnatural' about the uneven development of the north and the south of Ireland. In fact, this was part and parcel of how capitalism had spread its influence across the globe. Nor does it make much sense to deny the level of economic development which took place under British rule and condemn it as somehow unnatural or artificial. We need note only that this was a dependent development and one not based on the organic modernization of the country as a whole. Furthermore, we need not have naive hopes that alternative political arrangements – i.e. Irish independence – would have led to some spontaneous economic miracle. The structures of dependency were far too deeprooted for that and, anyway, it had created a substantial owning class in Ireland which benefited precisely from this subordinated mode of development.

In her overview of Irish social and economic history Mary Daly argues against the nationalist interpretation that even under an independent Irish parliament 'links between the two economies [Ireland and Britain] would have been very strong'[32] and that it is 'improbable that a substantially better outcome could have been possible'.[33] There appears to be some confusion in this argument which is only effective against rather simplistic nationalist view. Certainly it is not 'England' as such which thwarted Irish development but, rather, an unequal relationship with British capitalism. Elsewhere, Daly argues that the decline of milling in the eighteenth century was 'virtually independent of English competition, but was the product of changing technology or of the structure of farming'.[34] Yet how can we separate technological change or that in land-tenure systems from the influence of British imperialism? None of this means accepting that a simple imposition of tariffs would have sufficed, even though successful development cases have almost always used them. It is clear from our analysis that development prospects in Ireland were always conditioned, and more often determined, by the political, military, cultural and economic subordination to Britain. As to whether a better outcome would have been possible it is simply impossible to say with any degree of certainty.

Between 1916 and 1922 political events in Ireland unfolded with a dramatic intensity which completely overshadowed economic development. We have, however, grasped what type of economic structure and prospects Ireland had on the eve of independence. The partition of Ireland was to thwart may of those possibilities and, henceforth, we need to analyze the different developments in the South (Chapter 2) and North (Chapter 3) of Ireland respectively. Our basic framework of 'dependent development' has served as a useful tool of analysis. But we should not examine the Irish economy, or any other for that matter, as simple illustration of some grand theoretical schema. A recent book on the Irish economy after partition refers to it as being 'between two worlds'[35] referring to the advanced industrialized societies and the underdeveloped, so-called Third World. This description fits in well with the notion of dependent development employed in this chapter. Capitalism is a dynamic mode of production which tends to extend itself to all regions and all aspects of economic life. Capitalist development had reached a not negligible level in Ireland by 1920. It remained, however, a development dependent on Britain. It remains to be seen whether the new state would overcome this dependency.

2

The Southern Economy

Partition created two separate Irish economies in 1921. This chapter
deals with the 26 southern counties known as the Irish Free State and,
eventually, the Republic of Ireland. Having dealt with the effects of
partition in the previous chapter we deal here with the 26 counties as
an economic unit. We focus on the various phases of capital accumulation from the early stages of independent economic policy (1920–30),
the period of inward-oriented growth under De Valera (1930–50),
the following period of outward-oriented growth associated with Sean
Lemass (1950–70) through the oil crises of the 1970s to the 1980s and
current prospects for the Southern Irish economy. These economic
phases are also, of course, marked by social and political changes. That
is where our account will differ from the technical discussions of many
economists. To capture that integration of economic and social
processes we deploy the concept: 'regime of accumulation'. Essentially, it refers to a particular combination or articulation of production
and consumption. Rather than separating these two elements, as is
common in economic analysis, they are seen as a unified social process
within which social reproduction takes place. The associated term,
'mode of regulation', refers to the corresponding social and political
aspects which assure the relative stability of a regime of accumulation.
The hegemonic system which ensues – a class alliance based on consent
as much as coercion – sets the terms in which economic development
occurs.

Imperialist legacy

The various theories of imperialism, as applied to Ireland, have often
suffered from oversimplification. At times it seems that imperialism
refers to nasty things that Britain does to Ireland. Of course that does

not mean that imperialism is irrelevant. During the 'classical' age of imperialism Ireland fitted the Marxist theory perfectly as we saw in Chapter 1. Now, following the war of independence with Britain, we could expect the new 26-county Irish economy to develop a dynamic of its own. But the legacy of imperialism was a heavy one. As Joel Mokyr, not a nationalist economist by any means, argues, 'As the economy became more and more part of a larger economic unit (Britain and then the North Atlantic economy), it became more susceptible to exogenous disturbances which emanated from events in foreign countries.'[1] Mokyr is here referring to the Irish economy in the course of the nineteenth century, but the argument is equally applicable to the twentieth century. Ireland became in the 1920s a 'dependent' country defined as a situation where political independence is counterbalanced by continuing economic subordination. The small 'open' economy of the 26 counties faced an international system where it had no control over prices of either its inputs or the produce it wished to place on the international market. To say that an economy is particularly 'vulnerable to exogenous shocks' is but an academic way of describing the continued impact of Ireland's long history of imperialist domination.

Dependency and economic development are not incompatible. Industrialization can occur, even advances in per capita national product, but we still have dependent development. According to Bairoch's comparative study of European Gross National Product (GNP) per capita in 1912, Ireland was only a little below the average for Western Europe as a whole and over 50 per cent above the Eastern European level.[2] Does this mean that the economic links with Britain had been beneficial and had achieved a miraculous recovery from the dark days of the Great Famine of the mid nineteenth century? Ireland did in fact have a high per capita growth rate during this period (1850–1910). Partly this was due to a doubling of agricultural prices during this period, which was not matched by an increase in imported industrial goods. The other major explanation, of course, is that the population was nearly halved during this same period, which accounts for a *per capita* growth rate. We even find that per capita incomes rose during this period, but this is hardly surprising with the poorest half of the population being removed by emigration. As Kieran Kennedy notes, 'the improvement in Irish living standards in the second half of the nineteenth century is somewhat analogous to what happened in medieval Europe after the Black Death and the subsequent outbreak of bubonic plague'.[3] Population decline and specialization in well-priced livestock exports explain a seemingly favourable picture, not a genuine process of economic growth.

Economic historians like asking 'what might have happened?' in particular situations: this is the method of counterfactual history. An obvious question is thus whether Ireland's failure to industrialize prior to independence was inevitable. According to Michael Hechter, who has developed the notion of internal colonialism in relation to England's 'Celtic fringe', political sovereignty in the nineteenth century might have facilitated and encouraged economic diversification.[4] Irish industry might have survived had the state been in a position to erect trade barriers for its protection rather than submit to 'free-trade imperialism' with Britain. A more pessimistic view is taken by Joel Mokyr: 'Whether protective tariffs would really have made a substantial difference in Ireland's economic fortunes is, however, doubtful. It seems unlikely that government policies, of any type, could have brought about Ireland's much-desired industrialization.'[5] Certainly, the nationalist interpretation's emphasis on tariff protection, as the single instrument of industrialization, is adequate. Industrialization is, after all, a social process which entails a massive transformation of the whole relations of production. Ireland possessed adequate capital and labour supplies, as well as a communications network, even though coal and iron were lacking. However, having the resources necessary for industrialization could not overcome the obstacles created by military, and later economic, domination by Britain. Protective tariffs could hardly obliterate that legacy by themselves.

Returning to the economic history immediately prior to partition we must consider the effects of the First World War (1914–18). Dependency theorists such as Gunder Frank argue that industrialization in the periphery often occurs when there is a break in the international system either through war or a major international economic crisis. In the Irish context it is often said that 'in economic terms, the last years of the Union were the best ones'.[6] Agricultural prices trebled between 1910 and 1920, and so did the bank deposits of farmers. While exports boomed, there was a shortage of imports (due to the war) which, in turn, benefited the trader class. In manufacturing, the decline in foreign competition led to a significant recovery in several industries. As L.M. Cullen remarks: 'Farmer, trader and manufacturer did well. The urban and rural wage earner did less well, as wages lagged behind rising prices.'[7] So we find that the Gunder Frank thesis holds. That is to say, dislocation of the world market can create the conditions for development in a peripheral economy as self-sufficiency becomes a necessity. However, it was the agricultural sector which benefited more than industry. Furthermore, it was the owners of land and capital who benefited and not the population at large. It is precisely one of the characteristics of dependent development that it is export-led and does not lead to a balanced growth of a home market, which can only occur when the majority of the population achieve the economic wellbeing which allows them to become consumers.

The political party which controlled the first Dail in 1922 was Cumann na nGael (later to become Fine Gael) which had its main social base in the large farmers and the professionals of the city. Its main priority, after a debilitating civil war with the radical republicans, was to restore law and order and a semblance of stability in economic affairs. Independence was politically conditional and in any case incomplete, given the partition of Ireland. In the circumstances it was surprising that, as Kieran Kennedy notes, 'In restoring stability, the government was anxious to retain the goodwill and support of the British government.'[8] This precluded a concerted effort to protect Irish industry from cheap British imports. The British laissez-faire tradition in economic affairs was dominant among Irish economists. The government was more than prepared to accept their advice, being a product itself of a civil war against the uncompromisingly nationalist faction of the republican movement which had led the struggle against Britain. As British guns had facilitated their victory so Britain would not be inconvenienced by the new Irish government. Its objective, in which it was largely successful (eventually) was a conservative modernization of Ireland: a 'revolution from above' as it were, with decorum and without unleashing the powerful social forces which alone had made victory against Britain possible.

The overriding economic policy priority of the first 26-county government was undoubtedly agriculture. The logic was impeccable: Ireland was an agricultural economy, so to maximize the national income it was necessary to maximize farmers' incomes. The first Minister for Agriculture, Patrick Hogan, was to apply these objectives consistently and reject any lingering nationalist aspirations for self-sufficiency, let alone dangerous socialist ideas about reducing unemployment. However, this objective was subject to the changing conditions of the world market and dependency, once again, had its effects. Following the boom in agricultural prices during the First World War, they plummeted subsequently: from an index of 220 in 1920 to

160 in 1922 and 110 in 1931. The slogan of the time – 'One more cow, one more sow, one more acre under the plough' – was now impossible to achieve. So the government which wished to favour agriculture actually presided over its decline. Agricultural prices were not supported, agricultural education was not expanded, and agricultural loans were not provided, even though the Agricultural Credit Corporation was set up in 1927. The first decade of the Irish independence did, however, have some achievements in agriculture: standards were established for the testing, grading and packing of eggs, and measures were taken for the licensing of bulls for breeding!

Sinn Fein's Arthur Griffith had promoted the need for industrialization in the new Irish state. However, he, along with James Connolly the socialist leader, was now dead, and Sinn Fein anyway did not participate in the Dail. In the circumstances, the status quo prevailed. The Shannon electrification scheme, which began in 1925 and was completed in 1929, was an exception to the rule of failure to provide an adequate industrial infrastructure. In keeping with the academic opinion of the day, the government did not favour a large public sector, which would have been an absolute precondition for industrialization of a dependent economy. Nor did the government feel able to increase taxation to provide an industrial development fund. Farm incomes which were already exempt from taxation and tax rates, as a whole, were reduced from 25 per cent in 1924 to 15 per cent in 1927. Tariff protection to infant industries was granted very selectively and parsimoniously – applicants had to prove their case before a full public enquiry before an application would even be considered. However, as emigration declined in the early 1930s and under a threat of 'dumping' of goods from abroad, the pressure for a more aggressive protectionist stance became evident. Even before Fianna Fail (a Sinn Fein breakaway led by De Valera) assumed office in 1932, the inconsistencies and conservatism of the first Free State government were coming under pressure.

Inward-oriented growth

Ireland was not the only dependent economy to attempt an inward-oriented type of economic growth in the 1930s. The Great Crash of 1929 and the ensuing depression of the 1930s created the conditions in many underdeveloped countries for what became known as import-substitution industrialization. This involved, quite simply, producing at home industrial goods which had previously been imported. Thus economic necessity could lead to economic benefits in the long term as greater self-sufficiency was achieved. In Ireland it was paradoxically left to a British economist, Keynes, to provide the academic justification for the new turn towards protectionism. At a lecture held at University College Dublin in 1933, Keynes showed his sympathy with the new government's policy by saying: 'Let goods be homespun wherever it is reasonably and conveniently possible, and above all, let finance be primarily national.'[9] This advice was anathema to the dominant laissez-faire economists and, of course, to the ranchers and commercial interests in Ireland who had benefited from the link with Britain. However, with the trauma of the civil war being overcome the balance of political forces was changing. In 1932 the once uncompromising republicans of De Valera's Fianna Fail took office, supported by the small farmers, shopkeepers, artisans and workers generally, amidst a general nationalist fervour.

De Valera was elected on the basis that he would consistently apply the Sinn Fein ideal of self-sufficiency put forward by Arthur Griffith, and, most importantly, he pledged to abolish the land annuities still paid to Britain. These annuity payments collected from Irish tenant purchasers arose from the various Land Acts. De Valera argued that the annuities should go to the Irish Exchequer – the British government thought otherwise. When Fianna Fail withheld the first half instalment of 1932 (some £2.5 million) the British government responded with unexpected severity. The South's agricultural exports would be subject to a 20 per cent (soon raised to 30 per cent) duty on being imported to Britain. The Irish government, in turn, responded with a 'self-defence' Act which imposed duties on British coal, iron and steel goods amongst others. To a certain extent De Valera was using what became known as the Economic War to implement the protectionist path of economic development which he sought. Further duties were imposed on British goods in pursuance of this protectionist policy rather than in a spirit of retaliation. Undoubtedly the Fianna Fail government's stance on the matter of land annuities granted it considerable popularity which was to tide it over the often unfavourable consequences of the Economic War. Before it was over in 1938 this dispute was to set the basis for inward-oriented economic growth in the South of Ireland.

By 1936 the Dublin government had imposed tariffs on over 4,000 categories of imports, many ranging from 50 to 75 per cent. Other non-tariff barriers – such as import licences and quotas – were deployed to further protect the domestic market from foreign competition. Furthermore, the Control of Manufactures Act of 1932 ensured that in all new manufacturing companies, 51 per cent of shares should be in local hands. There was thus a range of measures taken to promote industrial self-sufficiency. Measures were also taken in agriculture to promote self-sufficiency with duties being levied on many agricultural products and subsidies being paid to Irish exports to Britain to overcome the effects of the Economic War. What we have is thus the combined effect of the Economic War and a consciously adopted set of protectionist measures. To this must be added the obviously unexpected effects of the international capitalist recession of the 1930s. By the time economic relations with Britain had been normalized through the 1938 agreement the Second World War was beginning. This was to produce another round of disruption for the Irish economy. The voluntary goal of self-sufficiency now became an imposed policy tending towards autarchy.

The combined impact of the international recession and the Economic War on Irish agricultural exports was severe as we see in Table 2.1.

Table 2.1: Irish Free State Exports (1931–5)

	1931	1932	1933	1934	1935
£ Million	36.3	26.3	19.0	17.9	19.9
Index of prices (1930: 100)	90.5	78.5	64.5	60.9	61.7
Index of volume (1926: 100)	98	82	74	72	77

Source: L.M. Cullen, *An Economic History of Ireland Since 1660*, London, Batsford, 1981, p.177.

By 1938, export prices had still not recovered their 1931 levels and, remarkably, the volume of merchandise exports of 1930 was not recovered until 1960. The big ranchers were less affected than the small dairy producers by the Economic War. The promise to fundamentally restructure Irish agriculture was thus not delivered. In fact, during the 1930s and 1940s there was a marked consolidation (concentration) of farms, especially in the east. In the west, poverty and emigration still prevailed. Certainly nothing was done to fulfil De Valera's stated objective 'to free the countryside from the dominance of cattlemen, to extend the area of tillage, to develop home industries and to provide employment for those who might otherwise be forced to emigrate'.[10] We must now consider whether progress was made on the industrialization front.

The bare statistics are that between 1931 and 1938 industrial production grew by a massive 50 per cent, while industrial employment increased from 110,500 to 166,000 over the same period or over 6 per cent per annum. However, industrial productivity did not grow, nor was much progress made in expanding industrial exports, with production being almost completely turned towards the internal market. Neither can the increase in industrial production be solely attributed to the protectionist measures: the housing boom of the 1930s must have accounted for a considerable proportion. The type of industrialization which occurred was also limited, concentrated as it was in the footwear, hosiery, glass, paper, leather, bricks and other such sectors. This was not heavy industrialization, the production of machinery which, in turn, could produce further industrial goods. The few manufacturing export industries which existed – such as brewing – in fact fared badly in the 1930s. An essential limit was posed by the internal market, which was not only small, but the national income in real terms was stagnant throughout the 1930s. Thus we find that the Gross National Product only rose by 10 per cent in the 1930s due, in particular, to a sharp decline in the terms of trade. Thus dependency was continuing to have its effect.

A precondition for industrialization in dependent economies is active state intervention to provide the essential infrastructure. Under the Fianna Fail government, state intervention did become more marked with 19 state bodies being formed between 1927 and 1939. These included the Electricity Supply Board (ESB), the Turf Development Board (later to become Bord na Mona), the Industrial Credit Company, Aer Lingus the national airline, Ceimici Teoranta a chemicals manufacturer, Comlucht Siucre Eireann to produce sugar from beet and, last but not least, the Irish Tourist Board (Bord Failte). Yet the South still had no shipping fleet of its own and thus relied on Britain for import supplies. During the Second World War British ships were withdrawn and, belatedly, Irish Shipping was formed to try to make good the shortfall. However, the key move in state promotion of industrialization came with the formation of the Irish Development Authority (IDA) in 1949. This state-sponsored body was initially charged with the administration of tariffs and quotas in specific industries, but in the

1950s its brief was extended to attracting foreign capital and encouraging new indigenous industry. Not entirely consciously, and certainly not from deep-held beliefs in the benefits of state intervention, the new Irish government was providing the essential framework for sustained self-sufficient economic growth.

To sum up, following Kieran Kennedy, we would argue that 'the strenuous protection of industry and agriculture in the 1930s had succeeded in changing only the nature but not the fact, of Ireland's dependence on the outside world'.[11] This is an important point because De Valera had argued that breaking economic dependence on Britain was an absolute priority, even if it meant a lower standard of living in Ireland. In fact, the Economic War was not used to achieve a substantial redirection of Irish trade away from Britain. In its aftermath it seemed as if it would be 'business as usual' as far as Anglo-Irish economic relations were concerned. Fianna Fail was no more consistent than Cumann na nGael had been in implementing the necessary measures to isolate the economy from the forces of international capitalism and attempt non-dependent development. Indeed, Arthur Griffith had himself originally seemed to suggest that US investment should substitute British investment. This was hardly a recipe for self-sufficiency. Meanwhile, the continued drain of labour persisted as emigration increased, particularly to fulfil Britain's labour needs during the Second World War. Fianna Fail had implemented a social rather than a socialist economic policy, with its innate conservatism and pragmatism always overriding any urges towards more radical changes, which might have received widespread popular support.

The De Valera era was crucial in providing the basis for a transformation of Irish society. This period, taken as a whole, can be described as a 'passive revolution' to use the term coined by the Italian socialist, Antonio Gramsci. He went on to describe 'molecular changes which in fact progressively modify the pre-existing composition of forces, and hence become the matrix of new change'.[12] It is a process of simultaneous revolution and restoration, in other words, a conservative revolution from above. De Valera effectively prepared the Southern part of Ireland to enter the age of monopoly capitalism, in spite of his dreams of a rural Arcadia marked by 'the romping of sturdy children, the contests of athletic youths and the laughter of comely maidens'.[13] Meanwhile, far away from this utopia, Fine Gael was entering a coalition with the leftist Clann na Poblachta (which reaped the benefits of popular discontent with the results of De Valera's economics) to

assume office in 1948. Already the seeds of an alternative economic
strategy had been sowed. Sean Lemass, who had devised most of the
key Fianna Fail economic policies from the 1930s to the 1950s, was
beginning to pose a new direction. Towards the end of the Second World
War, Lemass was complaining about the inefficiency of Irish farmers
and had even proclaimed openly to the Dail, the then heresy, that there
were too many people on the land.

Outward-oriented growth

The perceived failure of inward-oriented growth in the 1950s encouraged a sharp turn towards outward-oriented growth policies towards the
end of the decade. Again, Ireland was not unique and was following a
common Third World shift in this direction. Import substitution
industrialization appeared to be reaching its natural limits, having
exhausted the 'easy' stages of light industrialization. To begin home
production of footwear and textiles was one thing: a steel industry and
the production of machinery something quite different. Nor was the
home market of a size which could soak up the increased production
which would result from a qualitative leap forward in inward-oriented
growth. The international economic context had also changed.
Whereas in the 1930s most capitalist countries had turned towards
protectionism – and thus Ireland was no exception – in the buoyant
postwar economic climate open economies became the norm. The
capitalist world economy was entering the long postwar boom, a period
of unprecedented expansion. Trade had already internationalized
commercial and financial relations. Now production was becoming
internationalized. The bearers of these new international relations of
production were the transnational (or multinational) corporations,
primarily those from the United State. In the South of Ireland, a period
of economic euphoria and foreign takeover was about to commence.

The South of Ireland did not immediately enter this accelerated flow
of history. Indeed, during most of the 1950s the policy of protectionism
persisted, and little effort was made to re-orient towards the buoyant
European market. However, the considerable gains in terms of both
output and employment in the protected industries was not to be
repeated in the 1950s. Room for expansion was limited and imports
were gaining ground. As to agriculture, modernization had hardly made
an impact in a very conservative environment. Emigration continued to

highlight the failure of the Irish economy to provide a livelihood for its population. De Valera returned to office in 1957 in conditions when the economy had, in the words of government economist T.K. Whitaker, 'plumbed the depths of hopelessness'.[14] The old nationalist protectionist economic strategy had reached its limits. In 1958 a symbolic but nevertheless significant act was the abolishing of the 1932 Control of Manufacturers Act which, as we saw above, was designed to keep industry in Irish hands. Attracting foreign investment was now more important than nominal respect of nationalist sensibilities. The state had laid the infrastructural basis – and, of course, the essential social services such as housing and health – for capitalist expansion. Irish capitalists had neither the conditions (civil war followed by depression followed by war) nor, possibly, the inclination (Irish capital still flowed to Britain) to take advantage of it.

In retrospect the year 1958 marks a decisive shift towards outward-oriented growth, which was truly a new regime of accumulation with far reaching economic, social, political and cultural effects. This was the culmination of a process of reorganization by the capitalist classes of the South which had begun in the mid 1950s. The post-1958 incarnation of Fianna Fail was considerably different in its class composition from that of the 1930s: it now basically expressed a compromise between the old British-linked commercial interest and the newly emergent capitalist tied to US-dominated foreign investments. Sean Lemass took over leadership of Fianna Fail from De Valera, symbolizing the shift towards a new era. The 1958 Department of Finance document, *Economic Development* (actually written by T.K. Whitaker) expressed many of these tendencies arguing unequivocally that 'sooner or later, protection will have to go and the challenge of free trade accepted' insofar as 'there is really no choice for a country wishing to keep pace materially with the rest of Europe'.[15] This was a long way from De Valera's frugal vision and 'hairshirt economics'. Self-sufficiency was no longer an issue and borrowing abroad would be used to finance the new economic policy. Amongst all the debates and visions of a new Ireland a vital fact should be noted: it was in the 1950s that agriculture lost its role as the main employer of labour in the South.

Between 1958 and 1973 the Republic's terms of trade improved by nearly 40 per cent, thus giving a considerable boost to exports. Agricultural output, which had been more or less stagnant since the First World War, increased by 50 per cent. Foreign capital was attracted and manufactured exports grew at an average 23 per cent per annum between 1958 and 1973. Local firms also benefited as internal demand increased. Perhaps the most significant statistic of all is that between 1958 and 1973 industrial output increased two-and-a-half-fold. The Gross Domestic Product (GDP) arising from industry was nearly double that accounted for by agriculture. Even emigration began to fall after 1958 and by the early 1970s there was even a small net immigration. It appeared that a certain social and economic stability was being achieved by the new Irish state some 50 years after breaking politically with Britain. The South of Ireland was no longer a simple agrarian economy. Industrialization, urbanization and secularization were proceeding apace. For the first time in its history, practically, the population was increasing. It appeared that the South had thrown off its imperialist heritage and was ready to join the European Economic Community in 1973 as a fully equal partner with advanced European nation-states.

Outward-oriented growth, however, had certain implications. Internationalization of a small economy such as the Irish one and integration within the European and later world markets is a two-way process. Access to these markets for Irish agricultural produce or foreign-enclave produced manufactured goods, also implies access to the Irish market for others. As Raymond Crotty notes:

> Irish manufacturing industry was obliterated in the nineteenth century, when it first experienced free trade under factory capitalism. The fundamental structure and institutional flaws at the root of that persist; the economy continues to be small and isolated with a stagnant agriculture.[16]

In the new international division of labour which emerged in the postwar period, economies which had previously been agricultural and colonial began to industrialize. Nevertheless this was a subordinate type of industrialization – a typical form of 'dependent development' in fact. Nor was economic diversification and the reduction of traditional dependence on Britain that marked, at least until the 1970s, as we see from Table 2.2 on overseas investment.

There were serious structural weaknesses in the Irish economy even during the boom period. In spite of economic development total employment did not rise, as we see from Table 2.3 on employment trends. We note that the increase in industrial employment and the allied service sector did not compensate for the long-term decline in agricultural employment. Another aspect which concerned economists was the excessive reliance of the development model on the state sector,

Table 2.2: Overseas Investment in the Republic of Ireland (No. of Firms)

Country of origin	Period		
	Pre-1965	1965–9	1970–4
United States	27	20	69
United Kingdom	41	35	46
West Germany	14	12	33
Netherlands	8	4	8
Others	11	17	28

Source: IDA.

Table 2.3: Employment in the Republic (Thousands)

Year	Agriculture	Industry	Services	Total
1951	496	282	438	1,216
1961	360	252	405	1,017
1971	272	320	457	1,049

which carried out nearly 50 per cent of all investment. This was financed partly through increased taxation, which was of course unpopular. Furthermore the rise of inflation in the late 1960s caused considerable social unrest as workers and other social groups strove to maintain their relative positions. Moore McDowell refers to the fiscal crisis which hit the Republic after 25 years of steady growth in public spending:

> In the context of rapid economic growth, an expanding tax base makes growing public spending easy to accommodate politically. However, a stagnant, or declining level of real incomes per head means sharper political opposition to funding increased public sector activity.[17]

The liberal consensus of the 1960s regarding public spending was finally destroyed by the recession of the 1970s. The seeds of this conflict had, however, already been sown in this earlier period though not recognized.

The long 1958–73 boom did not produce a coherent dynamic capitalist class in Ireland, the 'bourgeoisie conquerante' of which Marx spoke admiringly. Kieran Kennedy writes of 'the comparative failure of indigenous private enterprise to respond to the incentives which had proved successful in attracting foreign enterprise' and more bluntly that 'there was no tendency in business towards greater self-reliance'.[18] We can assume that it was not a psychological problem – a lack of 'moral fibre' as it were. It is, rather, the history of dependency in Ireland which accounts for this failure. The link with Britain had encouraged the development of what is known as a 'comprador bourgeoisie' which refers to a capitalist class which is not really dependent but rather acts as an agent (buyer literally) for a foreign power. If in the nineteenth century the profits reaped from landownership went into London banks, now the Irish capitalist tended to invest profits in acquiring foreign businesses. Irish banking has always been very profitable, acting as a financial intermediary in this process. The Whitaker strategy of reintegrating Ireland into the world economy after 1958 only increased dependence. The 'economic take-off' which was planned for the 1960s was still crippled by dependency and never became translated into durable self-sustained economic growth. Genuine national economic development was neither intended nor achieved.

We have said that the shift from inward to outward-oriented growth represents a move towards a whole new 'regime of accumulation' around 1958. It entailed a turn from an extensive regime of accumulation, based on competitive regulation of the economy, to an intensive regime of accumulation, based on monopoly regulation. In the second phase any vestiges of a traditional way of life are swept away. Workers – now the largest section of the working population – become consumers and a vital element in the intensive development of industrialization. State intervention moved beyond the political sphere and the legal framework of economic activities, to embrace a broader economic role, countering the capitalist cycle and managing the reproduction of the whole social system. Competitive capitalism and agriculture began to give way to monopoly capitalism and services. There is also, of course, an international aspect to regulation. In Ireland, 1958 represented a shift from an ambiguous attempt at achieving a national mode of regulation to a frank acceptance of the hierarchy of international accumulation and the South of Ireland's subordinate role in that system. The mode of regulation of the Irish economy thus, once again, accepted the dominant role of the external context. However, industrialization produced a sizeable working class which developed a troublesome ability during this period to defend its living standards.

International economic crisis

While the international economic conditions were favourable, a small outward-oriented open economy could prosper. But with a succession of oil crises, 'stagflation' and a generalized recession within the world economy in the 1970s things began to change. The long postwar boom was coming to an end and the old economic recipes were losing their efficacy. If changing international conditions set the scene for the South's economic problems in the late 1970s and 1980s it is not the whole explanation. As Crotty remarks, 'The slowing down of the exceptionally rapid world economic growth, like the levelling off of a downward gradient, merely highlights the impossible defeats of the Irish economic vehicle.'[19] A particularly blunt symptom of this is the drop in the absolute number of people employed in the 1980s compared to the 1950s. By the mid 1980s one in five of the workforce was registered as unemployed and emigration was reaching 30,000 per annum. Not surprisingly in 1986, for the first time in 25 years, the total population of the Republic actually fell. This is the critical social backdrop to the series of economic problems which beset the Republic in the 1970s including a fiscal crisis, inflation and the rise of the foreign debt. During this period the condition of dependence was reinforced, even if it was 'diversified' away from the traditional British focus.

For an economy dependent on imports for nearly three-quarters of its energy requirements the tenfold increase in international oil prices in 1973 and 1979 came as a considerable shock. The balance of payments obviously suffered but it also generated inflation. The response of successive governments was to increase borrowing, thus abandoning the post-independence principle of always balancing expenditure and revenue. Reflecting the broad economic consensus shared by the major political parties, both the Fine Gael/Labour Party Coalition in power in 1973, and the Fianna Fail government of 1979, adopted similar measures in response to the oil price shock. However, as Kieran Kennedy notes:

> From a counter-cyclical viewpoint this was not the best time, given the public finance and balance of payments position, to boost demand still further. Moreover, the economy was now much more open than in the past, so that the impact of fiscal expansionism was likely to spill into imports more quickly and to a greater degree than heretofore.[20]

So the condition of dependence effectively precluded the traditional Keynesian methods of overcoming depression as the national economy was not effectively controlled by the national government. By 1982 the tide had turned effectively against Keynesianism and all the major political parties called for 'fiscal rectitude'.

Successive governments in the 1970s and 1980s presided over a gradual economic decline, in spite of the recovery between 1977 and 1979. Table 2.4 outlines the changes in the average annual growth rates during this period.

Table 2.4: Average Annual Growth Rates (1960–86)

	1960–73	*1973–9*	*1979–86*
Gross National Product (adjusted for terms of trade)	4.8%	2.2%	0.2%
Gross National Disposable Income	4.9%	2.8%	0.3%

Source: K. Kennedy et al, *The Economic Development of Ireland*, 1988, p.82.

We see that in the 1960s and early 1970s GNP and disposable income rose at a steady if unspectacular rate of nearly 5 per cent, this dropped to less than half that rate in the rest of the 1970s and was essentially reduced to zero for the 1980s. Even agriculture, after the initial boom on joining the EEC in 1973, began to suffer. These were, of course, international trends but the increased openness of the Southern Irish economy increased their impact. An indication of this susceptibility to outside pressure is the fact that the ratio of exports plus imports (goods and services) to GNP practically doubled – 73 per cent in 1972 to 138 per cent in 1985. This is a rough indication of the importance of the external economy compared with the national economy.

In terms of the mode of regulation, the main characteristic of this period was the failure to generate a stable pattern of employment. A self-sustaining industrial base had simply not been created by the post-1958 regime. Continuing the statistics from Table 2.3 we note in Table 2.5 the unemployment trend for the 1970s and 1980s.

Table 2.5: Employment in the Republic (Thousands)

	Agriculture	Industry	Services	Unemployment	Total
1971	272	320	457	61	1,049
1981	196	363	587	126	1,146
1986	168	301	606	227	1,075

From 1970 to the mid 1980s total employment remains static, while the population increased from 2.9 million to 3.5 million. The total number of unemployed, however, rose from 61,000 to 227,000 or nearly fourfold, over this same period. Agriculture continued its long-term decline, losing some 100,000 workers. The service sector expanded by some 150,000 workers, not all of those employed in the productive sector, however. The crucial industrial sector – key to any sustained development strategy – began to lose workers, not dramatically perhaps, but certainly this was a significant trend. De-industrialization was a worrying trend for an economy which had only in recent years begun to industrialize.

One of the major economic issues to emerge in the 1980s was the foreign debt. In 1981, the South's foreign debt was still less than the value of its exports. But this was hardly cause for any congratulation, reflecting as Crotty remarks, 'Ireland's greater dependence, as a small economy, on foreign trade, rather the scale of its foreign indebtedness'.[21] The latter had risen from £2,480m in 1973 to £23,045m in 1986. Since the Second World War the Republic's ratio of foreign debt to GNP had hovered around the 50 per cent mark. However, after 1973 borrowing increased substantially to finance the public capital expansion programme but also the current budget deficit. This fitted with the Third World experience of the time when massive borrowing took place. Interest rates were no longer as favourable (practically negative) as they had been in the past and by the 1980s the South was proving to be extremely vulnerable to its high debt/GNP ratio. As a result, between 1973 and 1986, the national debt/GNP ratio had risen by 90 per cent, which was considerably more than the increase in the whole of the previous history of the Republic. The scale of the Irish debt was simply enormous – over one-and-a-half times the GNP by 1987 – and no amount of reference to the Southern's state of credit-worthiness in comparison to the Third World debtor countries such as Brazil or Mexico could hide that fact.

Another major source of concern (for some) was the increased dependence on foreign investment which was highlighted in the 1980s by the decline of national industry. While foreign investment poured into the country economic statistics looked good, but when profits (unrestrained by any government measures) began to pour out the net advantage appeared questionable. The role of foreign manufacturing investment in terms of employment was certainly increasing during this period as we can see from Table 2.6.

Table 2.6: Foreign and Indigenous Manufacturing Employment (1973–85)

Source	Employment			
	1973	*1980*	*1985*	*1973–85*
Britain	26,932	22,652	14,100	–12,832 (47.6%)
US	14,935	32,563	36,500	+21,565 (144.4%)
Total foreign	58,892	81,968	78,373	+19,481 (333.1%)
Indigenous	158,400	166,300	134,857	–23,543 (14.9%)
TOTAL	217,292	248,268	209,841	–7,451 (3.4%)
% foreign	27.1	33.0	37.3	

Source: B. Brunt, *The Republic of Ireland*, London, PCP, 1988, p. 24.

From Table 2.6 we note firstly the continued decline (nearly 50 per cent) of British investment in the South and the concomitant rise of US (which multiplied nearly threefold) and other foreign investment. Perhaps just as significantly, the proportion of employment accounted for by foreign firms increased from 27 per cent of the total in 1973 to 37 per cent in 1985.

In viewing the 1980s we might consider the apparent contradiction between economic planning and political instability. Economic planning had been a hallmark of successive governments since 1958 with economic programmes following one after the other. This was indicative planning modelled loosely on contemporary French 'programming'. The strength of these plans lay in their ability to coopt labour through the trade union representation on the National Industrial Economic Council. By 1980 this move towards corporatism had even led to a National Understanding for Economic and Social Development involving the state, employers and trade unions. However, the very possibility of effective economic programming in an open economy must be questionable. The policies of transnational plants in Ireland are set by home offices in New York, Frankfurt or Tokyo and not in Dublin. Political instability in the Republic since 1973 – with Fianna Fail and Fine Gael alternating in government six times – has made the notion of economic planning even more problematic. For Fianna Fail the problem was particularly acute as Paul Bew and co-authors note:

> From 1979 the twin poles of its development strategy (state and private enterprise) entered into clear contradiction. It became increasingly difficult for the party to reconcile its role in the elaboration of strategies that would allow for the expanded reproduction of domestic and foreign capital and at the same time maintain its hitherto unchallenged hegemony over the working class.[22]

Finally, the 1980s marked a severe crisis in the intensive regime of accumulation established in the South of Ireland following the 1958 turn towards outward-oriented growth. With the onset of economic crisis in the 1970s and recession in the 1980s, consensus on economic matters evaporated. A regime of accumulation requires a stable balance between production and consumption. During the years of the economic boom and even in the early 1970s workers were able to defend their living standards. With a regime of 'fiscal rectitude' and the granting of free operation to market forces, social and political struggles intensified. The mode of regulation of the Southern Irish economy had entailed a form of corporatism and an avoidance of naked class struggle or even the language of class. National solidarity was hardly a credible appeal when the Dublin government took a passive role towards the intensifying crisis in Northern Ireland. In the mid 1970s Charles Haughey had declared that: 'We are not a rich community with large accumulations of private wealth crying out to be redistributed in the name of social justice.'[23] This seemed to set the seal on the crisis of the whole regime of accumulation which had prevailed since 1958. The owners and agents of capital in the South, along with their political representatives, were beginning to pursue a more openly capitalist line in politics.

Future prospects

As we enter the 1990s a brief retrospect on the Southern Irish economy is in order. Seventy years after the break with Britain how did the economy rate? After the troubled 1980s what are the future prospects of the Republic's economy?

The first and obvious question is whether independence from Britain actually benefited economically that part of Ireland which broke with Britain in the 1920s.

Table 2.7:
Real Product per Capita (Average Annual Growth Rate %)

	1926–85	1926–38	1938–50	1950–60	1960–73	1973–85
United Kingdom	1.7	2.0	0.9	2.1	2.6	1.1
Northern Ireland	2.0	0.6	3.5	2.2	3.1	1.0
Republic of Ireland	1.8	1.4	1.0	2.2	3.8	0.5

Source: K. Kennedy et al., *The Economic Development of Ireland*, p.118.

At the broadest level we can note that from 1926 to 1985 the comparative levels of growth were not dissimilar across the three regions, certainly well within the margin of error for this type of calculation. The Republic, however, is seen to perform best after 1958 when the historic links with Britain were loosened by diversification of trade relations. Northern Ireland fared best during the Second World War, a particular and artificial situation which we shall return to in the following chapter. Finally, the Republic is seen to go through a particularly marked recession following 1973, which reinforces the analysis of the preceding sections of this chapter.

The bare statistics of economic growth do not, however, show the changing social structure of the South consequent on industrialization. Table 2.8 outlines the broad sweep of the three main sectors of employment since 1926.

Table 2.8: Employment in the Republic 1926–86 (Thousands)

	1926	1936	1946	1961	1971	1981	1986
Agriculture	653	614	568	360	272	196	168
Industry	162	206	225	252	320	363	301
Services	406	415	432	405	457	587	606
TOTAL	1,220	1,235	1,225	1,018	1,019	1,146	1,075
Unemployed	79	96	64	59	61	126	227

Source: K. Kennedy et al., *The Economic Development of Ireland*, p.143.

As we have seen in previous sections there is a gradual and long-term decline in agricultural employment which by 1986 was a quarter of what it was in 1926. Industrial employment, for its part, barely doubled over the same period. As to services, the number of employed increased by 50 per cent. Neither industrial nor service sector expansion can mask the hard fact that 60 years of independence have led to a net decrease in employment and a trebling of unemployment rates. This is hardly a glowing picture but many of the weaknesses can be attributed to the difficulty in overcoming the inheritance of colonialism. A continuation of a more direct link with Britain would almost certainly have been worse for the Irish economy.

Having examined the overall economic record of the South and its changing socioeconomic structures, we can turn to the question of the social groups who came to dominate since the 1958 turn. Foreign firms now account for more than two in five of all manufacturing jobs, and this proportion is rising. This overall statistic masks the fact that in some industries the proportion is much higher: in chemicals 75 per cent of employment is in foreign-owned firms, in drink and tobacco the proportion is 70 per cent and in textiles 65 per cent. By the mid 1980s foreign-owned firms accounted for over half of the total turnover in Irish manufacturing. As Eoin O'Malley notes: 'The activities of Irish companies are noticeably lacking in the major high technology, capital intensive, large scale industries which would dominate the list of the largest companies in developed industrial economies.'[24] In the key industries such as electronics, chemicals, engineering or metals there are hardly any large Irish companies working independently of foreign firms. That banking and finance is in largely local hands does not compensate for this lack in the crucial productive areas. As to the prospects for national development in the South, Richard Stanton goes as far as to say that: 'There is no substantial local bourgeoisie awaiting its chance.'[25] Dependent development has created a dependent bourgeoisie quite unable to take over the leading role of the ranchers in an earlier historical phase.

Foreign investment can create development – albeit dependent – but it can also be withdrawn. That is precisely the problem with relying on multinational corporations as promoters of development. The branch plants they set up in Ireland during the 1960s and 1970s were characterized by the lack of forward and backward linkages with the rest of the economy, that is to say they were not integrated into the economy and remained 'enclaves'. Furthermore, inward investment was gained by the Southern Irish state at the price of a quite extraordinary set of incentives, including grants for fixed assets and zero tax on profits attributable to export sales. Profit repatriation (that is out of Ireland) by multinationals rose from I£258m in 1980 to I£1,275m in 1987. The Industrial Development Authority (IDA) promoted the role of Ireland as an 'export platform' into Europe and the provision of a cheap yet educated 'labour pool'. But as the Economist Intelligence Unit notes, 'A number of major multinational firms have reduced or closed their Irish operations in recent years. They have included recently established US firms and older UK firms.'[26] Global restructuring by these firms obviously did not consider the national development needs of Ireland. So, not only are the multinationals of dubious benefit to the Irish economy – in terms of creating a sustainable and developed pattern – but they are also prone to abrupt withdrawal, often after having reaped all the financial benefits made available by the state.

Dependent development is also uneven, both in geographical and social terms. A study of spatial planning in Ireland by Helen O'Neill concludes that: 'The country is a colonial or neo-colonial-type economy with strong centre-periphery relationships operating both externally and internally.'[27] Both Dublin and Belfast are seen to operate as a centre within the respective states, dominating other towns and the rural areas.

This is true in both economic and political terms, and is reflected in population movements towards these centres. Moves have periodically been made to reverse this spatial division of labour but have tended to be dropped when state-level development became a major political issue again. Thus the whole territory of the Republic is designated as an underdeveloped region by the European Community. With the escalating foreign debt the creation of greater regional equality ceased to be a major concern. Multinationals did often invest in peripheral areas – both in the South and the North – but, as we have seen, this investment was notoriously footloose. With increased international-ization of the Irish economy the two main urban centres of Dublin and Belfast have increased their roles as 'gateways' into their respective territories in terms of investment, transport, communications and technological advances. Certainly the spatial division of labour within Ireland has changed since the 1920s but it has not become more equal.

Another aspect of uneven development in Ireland is a curious blend of the old and the new, tradition and modernization. The latter has now come to be seen as the dominant trend at least since the 1960s. Yet the abortion and divorce referendums of the 1980s show that traditional values in the South are far from dead. (We can assume likewise for the North of Ireland.) The IDA is particularly adept at 'selling' the South in terms of its unique blend of the traditional and the modern. Without a hint of contradiction the location of factories (and pollution) is now set in the idyllic rural setting advertised by Bord Failte. A dolmen becomes an attractive image to sell digital computers, Newgrange nicely sets off the attractions of the Bank of Ireland. There is an underlying assumption that Ireland might miss out the horrors of industrialization, insofar as this has occurred late compared to its neighbour. In this new Japan of the West, pre- (or post-) modern values related to the family, weak collective organizations and deference to authority would come to the fore and provide the basis for renewed modernization. As Luke Gibbons, after considering the scenario said, 'The IDA image of Ireland as the silicon valley of Europe may not be so far removed after all from the valley of the squinting windows.'[28] This is a scenario we need to return to in our concluding chapter.

Having reviewed the salient features of Irish economic development we need to consider more directly its future prospects. A survey by the Economist Intelligence Unit states that: 'The macroeconomic outlook for the Irish economy by 1992 is for a return to modest GDP growth.'[29] It is believed that a continuation of present economic policies will also lead to a 'stabilization' of the debt/GNP ratio. Ominously, the report argues however that: 'Unemployment will continue to rise, and may reach 23 per cent of the labour force in 1992 unless emigration, already high, increases further.'[30] These forecasts assume, furthermore, that stabilization and growth will be the trend for the world economy. Any slowdown in world growth rates would seriously affect the growth's export expansion programme and would, likewise, reduce both consumer demand and employment. A more straightforward and pessimistic scenario is painted by Raymond Crotty, who believes the crisis is structural and probably terminal:

> Borrowing has papered over the fundamental flaws in the economy . . . the flaws which in the past caused half the population to starve or emigrate . . . But now too Irish society has been forced into dependence on foreign resources as complete as that of the exotic potato 140 years ago . . . Then mass famine ensued; now utter economic, political and social collapse will be the consequence.[31]

That is seen as the dire prospect if foreign credit is withdrawn.

We could speculate on the relative credit-worthiness of the Irish Republic compared to Third World debtors. By most accounts this is high. There is also an underlying resilience in the Irish economy which makes the totally bleak scenario realistically unlikely. That does not mean that the Economist Intelligence Unit scenario is a benign one as we shall examine further in Chapter 6. A fundamental omission in both optimistic and pessimistic scenarios alike is the question of partition. The Economist refers coyly to this: 'Another potentially destabilising factor is the problem of Northern Ireland' but finds that: 'Nevertheless, in day to day terms the Republic has remained largely insulated from the problems of the North.'[32] This may not, however, continue to be the case. In spite of the growth of what is known as '26-county nationalism' the South remains part of an unresolved national question. This is unlikely to fade away. The scenario of '1992' implies a crisis for small-nation nationalism but it also implies a need for the new supra-national European state to resolve its surviving national disputes. To discuss the prospects of the Southern Irish economy in isolation from these broader political issues may prove to be artificial. For the purposes of presentation we have examined the Southern, and in Chapter 3 the Northern, economy separately, but in reality their fates are inextricably intertwined.

3

The Northern Economy

The Northern Irish economy was quite distinctive, even before partition in 1920. We have already examined in Chapter 1 the basis of partition in the uneven development of the economy North and South. It is not the purpose of this chapter to delve further into the historical debates on the origins of industrialization in the North, but simply to outline its economic history since partition. A brief introductory section does, however, outline the basis of the North's industrial revolution and its integration with the British economy prior to partition. We then move on to a consideration of the staple economy, based mainly on shipbuilding and linen, in the 1920s, the 1930s and the Second World War. We then trace out the changes in the structure of employment during the postwar period as the staple industries began a long decline. As we move into the present period, one section deals with the economy during the 1970s and 1980s including the effects of the so-called 'Troubles'. Finally, we explore the current crisis in its main aspects, including the decline of the shipyard, the devastation of West Belfast and the so-called 'jobs crisis'. Advancing on our conclusions, we find that the Northern Ireland economy has now entered a period of apparently terminal crisis. Some of the available options or alternative scenarios are examined in Chapter 7.

Industrial revolution

By the mid nineteenth century, Belfast had become established as a leading provider of machine-woven linen and its second major industry, iron shipbuilding, was being set up. The linen industry was already well established, having been the leading sector of the Ulster economy since the turn of the century, encouraging a significant development of rural industrialization. In the 1850s it was beginning to stimulate the growth

47

of a Belfast engineering industry, which was becoming part of Britain's imperialist drive overseas. With the advent of power-loom weaving, the industry began to move towards large urban factories. The international economic downswing of the 1870s temporarily checked the development of linen but this was reversed in the 1890s when Ulster participated in Britain's export-led boom. As to the shipbuilding industry, it was not in its early years a dynamic leading sector of the economy. However, between 1870 and 1910 the labour force in this sector increased fivefold, as Belfast became a key provider of ships for Britain's free trade imperialism. An overall index of Belfast's 'great leap forward' is its doubling of population between 1880 and 1910. Of course, as John Othick notes, 'It is one thing to become effectively incorporated within a national economy which enjoys international pre-eminence; it is, however, a rather different matter to become an integral part of a national economy whose fortunes are in decline.'[1]

For the time being, prosperity of the leading sectors was creating a considerable degree of diversification, essential if any economy is to be durable and integrated. As J.M. Goldstrom writes:

> Linen and shipbuilding were the dominant industries of the north-east . . . But Belfast had many other industries, too, most of them springing up to meet the needs of these two giants. Spinning machines, scutching and hackling equipment were made in the city. So were steam engines, foundry products, ropes and heating and ventilating equipment. Manufacturers diversified and produced tea-drying equipment, stable fittings, agricultural machinery, motor cars, mineral waters and cigarettes.[2]

On the face of it, this was a veritable industrial revolution. Inter-industry links seemed to be well established, and the 'take off' into self-sustaining growth appeared to have been achieved. This pattern of industrialization, albeit dependent on Britain, appeared even more remarkable when set against the de-industrialization which occurred in the rest of Ireland during most of the nineteenth century. Even the (predominantly Protestant) industrial working class shared the Unionist political orientation of the employers, and were not likely to take industrial or political action which could jeopardize industrial relations or the state. The development of capitalism in the northeast of Ireland appeared to have achieved a particularly felicitous blend of the 'factors of production'.

Outside of Belfast, this favourable picture was not so widespread. In

Derry there was a thriving shirt-making industry, tobacco was processed and a few ships were built. Elsewhere we find but a few spinning mills, distilleries and flour mills. As Goldstrom concludes: 'The Ulster that lay beyond Belfast had more in common with the rest of Ireland than it had with its principal city.'[3] The rural industries which had sprung up during the early phases of industrialization were, by the second half of the nineteenth century, in open decline. Thus, uneven development at the national level had its counterpart within Ulster, where industry became concentrated in the northeast while the rest of the province suffered from de-industrialization. Thus, for example, mechanized spinning gravitated towards the northeast, while the rest of the region maintained handloom weaving. Eventually, even this level of industry was to decline. As Othick notes in this regard, 'It is a familiar theme in economic history that regions which were at a disadvantage vis-a-vis core industrial areas were often able to compensate by establishing a dominant relationship with regions even less favourably placed than themselves.'[4] In this context, the industrialization of the northeast could not provide an impulse for the organic development of the rest of Ireland.

The Northern Irish economy was, as we have already indicated, subject to fluctuations in the international capitalist economy. The so-called 'long waves' of the world economy led to periods of upswing between 1789 and 1815, from 1849 to 1873 and from 1896 to 1920. In between, of course, there were periods of downswing, characterized by relative stagnation. The North's prospects were thus determined by the cycles of the world economy and Britain's role in the international division of labour. Ulster had an ambivalent relationship with Britain as Othick notes: 'On the one hand, Britain represented a major potential source of the inputs of capital and technology necessary to revolutionize production; on the other hand, British competition represented a major backwash effect hindering the progress of manufacturing elsewhere.'[5] This backwash effect was, of course, felt most strongly during the cyclical downswings as British competition hindered development in Ireland. With the Act of Union of 1800 and the ratification of partition in 1920 the North's industrialists hitched their fates, as subordinate partners, to Britain's economy. Not quite a full economic region of the United Kingdom, isolated from the rest of Ireland, and unable to act as a national economy, Northern Ireland's economic prospects were always dependent on others.

There were serious limitations to the type of industrialization which had occurred in the northeast from the mid nineteenth century to the First World War. In the first place, this was dependent industrialization and was not based on the organic development of the Irish economy. As we have just seen, the fluctuations of the world capitalist economy had an overwhelming effect on the small export-oriented Northern Irish economy. Following partition, as Kennedy notes, 'Unlike the Republic, Northern Ireland was unable to impose tariffs or quotas, to conclude trade agreements with other countries, or to establish its own military and exchange rate policies.'[6] Without recourse to any of these measures Northern Ireland was totally subject to the vagaries of the much larger British economy. Once Britain's imperialist hegemony was questioned during the First World War, and completely shattered by the 1930s depression and the Second World War, the benefits of empire to Belfast and the skilled Protestant working class began to wane. Over-specialization of the North's industry was but one aspect of this region's total dependence on Britain. After 1920, while the rest of Ireland at least broke its political dependence, Northern Ireland became even more subordinate in economic, political and strategic terms to Britain.

The other major limitation of industrialization in the northeast was the failure to create a domestic market which could make it self-sustaining. Low wages and a declining population were not conducive to the development of a dynamic home market. Over-specialization has as one of its main symptoms a lack of domestic diversification and coherence, which in turn prevents the development of a national economy. Other small export-based economies, such as Denmark for example, have achieved this type of breakthrough. In these cases, there was invariably a far more even distribution of land and income. As economist Dieter Senghaas argues, 'Smallness as such does not have to result in a narrowness of the domestic market. The latter emerges only in the specific circumstances of a markedly unequal resource distribution.'[7] Northern Ireland was practically a textbook example of export-led growth, but lacked an orientation towards development of the home market. The 'labour aristocracy' of the North was far too limited to provide a viable home market. Essentially, of course, partition finally cut off any prospects of development for a coherent and viable Irish economy, based on a steadily increasing standard of living of its population.

Industrialization in the northeast of Ireland obviously created distinctive social and political interests. The owners of industry in that part of Ireland would not seek protectionist measures as their counterparts in the South should, insofar as they were integrated with the then dynamic British economy. Remaining part of the British free-trade area was essential to the economics of Unionism. As F.S. Lyons notes, 'In the six counties Unionism was the political creed not only of the gentry, not only of many businessmen, lawyers, doctors and Protestant clergy, but of a substantial number of farmers, agricultural labourers and industrial workers as well.'[8] The particular economic position of the North vis-a-vis the rest of Ireland provided an ideological cement which cut across social classes and consolidated the Unionist bloc. Quite inseparable from Unionism were the social consequences of imperialism or 'social imperialism'. Basically, part of Ireland's northeast was integrated into Britain's imperialist expansion overseas. The benefits from this which trickled down to the dominated classes may have seemed meagre in absolute terms but, in the Ireland of the Great Famine, the relative advantage was considerable. Nationalists probably underestimated the strength of these ideologies and certainly did not develop a coherent economic policy towards the northeast. There was no historical inevitability to partition and a free-trade orientation in the North.

A staple economy

The Northern economy had been based on the staple products of linen and ships for a considerable period. On the face of it, this made the region a suitable candidate for success according to the 'staple theory of economic growth' developed by Canadian economic historians.[9] Essentially this theory conceives of economic development as a diversification process evolving around an export base. For this to occur the export sector needs to establish linkages with the rest of the economy, both 'backwards' into agriculture, for example, and 'forwards' into industrialization. Furthermore, demand linkages need to be established internally with the demand for capital and consumer goods being induced by export earnings. Finally, fiscal linkages are essential for tariffs, duties and export taxes to be channelled back into domestic economic development. In the North of Ireland, prior to partition, there was a limited development of backward and forward linkages in the linen industry for example. However, the restricted development of a domestic consumer market made the 'demand linkages' mentioned above difficult to establish. With the Northern six counties remaining under British control after partition in 1920, the 'fiscal linkages' referred to were out of the question. It would therefore appear that the North of Ireland is a case of frustrated staple economic development which led inevitably to the decline of these staples products as we shall see.

When the state of Northern Ireland was established following partition, the British exchequer conceived of the region as yet another part of the British Empire and thus subject to the 'imperial contribution'. The North was expected to generate more wealth than it consumed, with the surplus accruing to the British state to assist in the military and other costs of Empire. In practice the new state's contribution began to rapidly dwindle, until in 1938 the British government recognized that henceforth it would have to subsidize the North. Pro-Unionist economists, such as Tom Wilson, refuse any negative connotation in Northern Ireland's failure to achieve fiscal self-sufficiency, rejecting any accusations of 'dependency' or of 'spongers', and arguing that 'over much the greater part of its half century of legislative devolution, the Province was treated less favourably than comparable regions in Great Britain'.[10] This does not, however, account for the long-standing resentment of the British Treasury which, along with prominent British politicians, viewed the North's Protestants as 'spongers' and described its politicians' financial demands as 'incredible if they were not in black and white'.[11] The point to be made is a simple one: the new state of Northern Ireland was not, and could not be, financially independent and from its inception was destined to a future of economic dependence on Britain.

From the outset, Northern Ireland had a very different economic structure from the rest of Ireland. Table 3.1 gives an overview of employment sectors in 1926.

Table 3.1: Sectoral Employment, 1926 (%)

	Agriculture	Industry	Services
Northern Ireland	29	34	37
Rest of Ireland	65	10	25

We see clearly here the divergence of economic structures caused by uneven development, which resulted in a relatively industrialized North (although agriculture still accounted for nearly one-third of employment), and a South where fully two-thirds of the population were still employed in agriculture. What these statistics do not show, however, is the extremely high level of unemployment prevalent in Northern Ireland since its inception. The unemployment rate averaged around 15 per cent during the 1920s but, with the onset of the international capitalist recession it almost doubled to reach 28 per cent in the early 1930s. The linen industry, which had employed almost 87,000 people in 1924, had only 61,000 workers a decade later in 1934. The shipbuilding industry reached a staggering 57 per cent unemployment rate in 1932, and one of the two yards (Workman Clark) closed never to open again. The acute dependency of the North made the effects of the international recession all the more severe and lessened its capability to recover.

The international recession of the 1930s affected Northern Ireland more severely, and for a more prolonged period, than the rest of the United Kingdom. The staple products of linen and ships were particularly hard hit during the interwar period. Whereas the British economy began to recover in the mid 1930s based on a modernization of the industrial base, as well as housebuilding, no such recovery occurred in Northern Ireland. By comparison the Southern economy (see Chapter 2) was relatively less affected by the international recession. This was because of the protection afforded by tariff barriers and its much greater orientation towards the domestic as against international markets. Ironically, agriculture in the North probably fared better, as it took good advantage of the protectionist and market-regulation measures introduced in the UK. The reduction in the amount of food imports into Britain during the 1930s was exploited in Northern Ireland. Thus, the Agricultural Marketing Act of 1933 led to the expansion of pig production in the North and even to a change of breeds which allowed the export of lean bacon, previously provided by Denmark, to the south of England. But increased production of pigs, lean or otherwise, could hardly compensate for the catastrophic decline of the shipbuilding and linen industries.

The Northern Ireland government did make some attempts at economic diversification during the 1930s, with the New Industrial Development Acts of 1932 and 1937 for example. These Acts provided for interest-free loans and grants to new industrial enterprises. But, as Kennedy notes, 'the powers were limited, however, and failed to have much impact'.[12] Indeed, the only notable result in the North was the establishment of an aircraft factory in 1937 by Short Brothers and

Harland. Part of the problem, of course, was that Northern Ireland was but one depressed region among many in the UK. Industries producing durable consumer products and services would naturally turn towards the populous and relatively well off south of England rather than to the distant and impoverished North of Ireland. Even pro-Unionist historian Patrick Buckland is driven to conclude that: 'Neither in the short nor the long terms did the 1930s new industries legislation do much to broaden Northern Ireland's industrial base or alleviate unemployment.'[13] Dependence once again seems to have thwarted any possibility of diversification, and certainly any prospect of self- sustaining growth. International conditions can explain the context of the 1930s crisis but not its particular mode of resolution, or its failure.

There was a recovery of Northern Ireland's economic fortunes during the Second World War (1938–45), a fortuitous event for local business. Ships and other military supplies could be provided by Belfast's staple industries and the Shorts aircraft factory would employ over 30,000 people at its wartime peak. Even the linen industry, which saw half its workforce unemployed at the outbreak of hostilities, could be reoriented to produce wartime supplies of clothing. Agriculture too saw a marked increase in output as the sector strove to take advantage of the wartime market. Increased production all round meant a decrease in unemployment. As an overall indicator of living standards we can note that, whereas before the war the North's income per head was less than three-fifth's that of Britain, by the end of the war the ratio had risen to three-quarters of the British level. Unionist leader Sir James Craig proudly declared that 'We are all King's men' as he put the resources of the North behind Britain's war effort. That this was not, however, an ordinary part of the UK was signalled by the British government's reluctance to apply conscription in Northern Ireland.

The Second World War may have provided a stay of execution for the North's shipbuilding industry, but it could not conceal the cracks in the economic foundations of the six-county state. Patrick Buckland admits that: 'The war brought about an increased awareness of just how underdeveloped Northern Ireland was in comparison with Britain.'[14] This was not just in terms of social conditions, housing and hygiene, however. Postwar scarcities continued, for a few years, to provide a market for the North's staple products. Yet this could not hide the fact that the postwar boom was based purely on outside factors. The industries of the North dated from an age of imperialism now past. Britain, one of the victorious allies in the war, nevertheless emerged as a second-rate economic power. Imperialism was now dying – at least in its classic British variant – and its economic outpost in the North of Ireland shared in this decay. A brutal fact to come was that there was to be no increase in manufacturing employment during the 1950s and 1960s. The long-term decline of shipbuilding was the most salient feature of this decline: whereas in 1948 the UK produced around half of the world's tonnage, by 1976 this proportion had dropped to less than 5 per cent.

We can now sum-up Northern Ireland's economic development in its first 25 years of existence. Tom Wilson, the Unionist economist already cited above, attempts to reject any accusation of dependency and argues that:

> Ulster's apparent financial weakness was seized upon by Irish nationalists as evidence that the Province was not economically 'viable' . . . [and] It was then inferred that, if only Britain would stop paying these subsidies, Northern Ireland would be obliged to abandon its resistance to unity with the south.[15]

For him, Northern Ireland was just as 'viable' as the new Irish Free State. This was simply not the case, as the ever-increasing economic subsidy to the North testified. Certainly, there would have been no automatic embrace between Unionists and Nationalists with the withdrawal of the subsidy. The real point is the one made by Paul Bew and co-authors, in the context of the early clashes between the British Treasury and the Unionist regime, namely, that: 'Had the Treasury objections [to Unionist 'profligacy'] been sustained in full, life would have been made almost impossible for the Belfast regime.'[16] We reach now the limits of a purely economic analysis, because the formation of Northern Ireland is tied up in a complex web of political, social and military struggles which cannot be reduced to the issue of its economic viability.

The postwar period

As Northern Ireland entered the postwar period, so the inherent fragility of its economic structures became more apparent. The shipbuilding and textile industries were once again in difficulties as dependence and lack of diversification took their toll. There were significant changes within these sectors, in particular the rise of the artificial fibres industry, but

what is noticeable is the continuation of specialization. This is clear in
Table 3.2 which examines the employment trends of four major
industrial sectors.

Table 3.2: Manufacturing Employment, 1952–71(%)

Sector	1952	1959	1971
Food, drink and tobacco	11.4	11.9	15.2
Textiles, clothing	51.2	46.6	38.7
Ships and marine engineering	11.6	13.0	5.5
Total	88.5	88.7	81.0

Source: K. Isles and N. Cuthbert, *Economic Survey of Northern Ireland*, Belfast,
HMSO, 1967, p. 63.

Shipbuilding was gradually marginalized by the broader engineering
sector but, overall, we note that in the 1950s specialization actually
increased, whereas in the 1970s concentration only decreased from
88 per cent to 81 per cent. This was precisely the period in which the
Southern economy was beginning to reap some of the benefits of
increased diversification.

The overall structure of employment in Northern Ireland mirrored
the changing pattern of accumulation in the postwar period; as we see
in Table 3.3.

Table 3.3: Sectoral Employment, 1926–71(%)

	1926	1961	1971
Agriculture	29	16	11
Industry	34	42	42
Services	37	42	47

Table 3.3 shows dramatically the long-term decline of agricultural
employment (see Chapter 5), the increase share of industrial employment which then, however, stabilized and the steady increase in

service-sector employment. This pattern of development bears some resemblance to that of other medium-sized semi-industrialized countries. The growing capital intensity of agriculture was everywhere displacing farmers. There was a healthy overall increase in industrial employment – and we must recall that in 1971 the South had only 25 per cent of the working population in this sector. Services, finally, had expanded to nearly half of the total, but this was not yet the bloated, dominating sector which it was to become. One problem deriving from dependency was, however, the high proportion of exports in relation to GNP: this was 70 per cent for the North in the mid 1960s, but only 25 per cent for the South and 14 per cent in the UK.

The steady growth of the service sector needs to be disaggregated if we are to understand its significance. As the British National Health Service was gradually, and often reluctantly, extended to Northern Ireland in the postwar period, so employment in the public services such as health and education could be expected to expand. Another particularly important sub-sector in the North was to become public administration and defence. But the service sector also has a private element including banking and distribution as well as hotel and catering. The service sub-sector which has been particularly weak in Northern Ireland, as Liam O'Dowd points out, is producer service activity such as public relations and financial services within industry.[17] Furthermore, the expansion of the service sector has been unduly concentrated in the Belfast area, which has absorbed well over half of all jobs created in this sector. Service-sector expansion has thus mirrored the spatial distribution and uneven development of manufacturing. The minority Catholic population did benefit from the expansion of the service sector – which did not maintain the tight exclusion practised by the heavy engineering industry for example – though they remained under-represented in the higher grades as shown by the 1971 census.

If local industries were declining, as we saw above, the increased significance of industrial employment has to be accounted for by the rise in foreign investment during the postwar period. During the 1950s and 1960s ICI, Dupont, Michelin, Cortaulds, Goodyear, ITT and many other transnational corporations opened branch plants in Northern Ireland. This was undoubtedly becoming the most dynamic sector of the economy. Yet it was a fragile basis for self-sustaining growth, in large part due to the branch-plant structure of these operations, which could leave as easily as they came in. Tom Wilson, an economic planner of the period, argues that 'everyone was aware of their vulnerability, but there was also a great belief, later to be rudely shattered, that slumps of any real severity would be avoided by Keynesian measures'.[18] For the time being the positive aspects seemed to prevail: between 1958 and 1975 employment in foreign-owned companies increased from 4,515 to 26,141, with more than three-quarters of these jobs being in plants of over 500 employees. These largely US-based companies concentrated their investment in the mechanical-engineering and textile sectors, thus not fundamentally altering the composition of the economy. Nor were there significant forward or backward linkages established by the foreign firms with the rest of the economy, which could have created a more durable platform for economic growth.

There is considerable debate on the location policy followed by the Stormont government in relation to foreign investment in the North. Bob Rowthorn and Naomi Wayne support the nationalist case that: 'In the 1950s and 1960s most new investment in the province went to the Protestant areas around Belfast: Antrim, Down and North Armagh. Relatively little went to the city of Belfast itself, or to Catholic areas of the province.'[19] Unemployment in predominantly Catholic towns was always much higher than in more 'Protestant' areas. The decline of nationalist Derry in the 1960s, compared to the nearby Unionist market town of Coleraine, was only formalized by the quite unjustified siting of the New University of Ulster in the latter. Yet Tom Wilson, who rejects the accusation of discrimination, can cite in his favour a Fair Employment Agency report which finds that: 'On the basis of our analysis of the distribution of projects and employment in relation to population there would seem to be no grounds to question the fairness of industrial development policy on the basis of religion.'[20] We cannot go into the methodology of this study here but only note that discrimination or unfairness in industrial location policy need not be proven; the issue is rather whether it fundamentally altered the uneven development of the North or the severely disadvantaged position of Catholics, and in this respect a negative answer is nearly universal.

There is no doubt that the role of the state in economic affairs increased dramatically in the postwar period. Tom Wilson recalls that:

When our work on a development programme started in the mid-1960's 'economic planning' was very much in vogue in Britain. That ambiguous term was then taken to mean 'indicative planning' after the model that appeared to have been used with some success at the national level in France.[21]

But Northern Ireland was not an integrated national economy, merely a peripheral region of an economy which itself was in long-term decline. The Wilson Plan of 1965 lacked any serious economic calculation, though it was an advance on previous piecemeal policies. It worked within the 'growth centres' framework and called for the creation of a modern economic infrastructure. The problem, however, was that state planning of any sort was inimical to the Unionist establishment. Not unsympathetic observers, Bew, Gibbon and Patterson refer to 'the blatantly cosmetic character of O'Neillist planning' and argue that: 'Planning merely represented, in a phrase which evidently pleased O'Neill, "stealing Labour's thunder".'[22] International experience has shown that a vigorous state intervention in economic affairs is absolutely indispensable for overcoming underdevelopment. In the North, a ruling class totally subordinate to the ideology of Empire was unable to implement the sort of radical measures which, albeit hesitantly and unevenly, were at the time being undertaken in the South.

We have already referred to the significant shift in the regime of accumulation in the South around 1958 (see Chapter 2). Was something similar happening in the North? The watchwords of this period were rationalization and concentration. This was the reality behind the ideology of modernization. The 1960s do appear to mark a shift in the mode of regulation of the Northern economy, but there does not seem to be a watershed as clear cut as 1959 was in the South. Nor was there a lucid ruling-class project comparable to the Lemass and Whitaker initiatives in the South. Though there was talk of 'transforming the face of Ulster', the Unionist leaders were far too conservative to initiate anything so radical. The transformation was piecemeal, it was not launched by a bold initiative from above, but it was still occurring. Traditional, extensive industrialization was being replaced by a more intensive industrialization based on a capital-intensive exploitation of labour rather than the crude policy of low wages on which the linen industry had been based. Workers were becoming consumers and not simply factory hands. The role of the state was increasing even if the governments of the day were less farsighted than their Southern counterparts and might even at times have seen it as creeping socialism.

The similar pattern of capital accumulation in the South and North of Ireland by around 1970 gave rise to a theory of 'convergence' between the two economies. The clear implication was that if the economies were growing closer together – sharing problems as much as successes – then the political barriers might too begin to fade. Rational economic debate would displace the irrational discourses of nationalism and sectarianism. This theory – or political wish – needs to be tackled in sections. Convergence between the two Irish economies had undoubtedly increased by 1970, compared say to 1920. What is more dubious is the notion of multinational capital as above politics and thus an unsullied agent of progressive change in the North. As Bew, Gibbon and Patterson note: 'All the bourgeoisie, all its fractions, wanted to maintain Stormont.'[23] There simply was no split between a progressive foreign capital and a reactionary domestic capital sector. At the heart of this theory is a fairly crude economism which argues that capital, being rational, gender-blind and, of course, not having a religion, could overcome divisions within the North and, ultimately, create the conditions for a peaceful reunification of Ireland. However, in practice, politics have a stubborn tendency to resist economic logic. This was never more true than when the North erupted once again in open political conflict in the 1970s.

The troubles and the economy

It is commonplace among political commentators to attribute a major role to political violence when assessing the economic ills of the North in the 1970s and 1980s. Bob Rowthorn and Naomi Wayne even produce figures on the effects of the conflict on employment – manufacturing losing 46,000 jobs between 1970 and 1985 whereas government services gained 36,000 jobs, thus a net loss of 10,000 jobs.[24] Yet we find other authors, such as David Canning et al., arguing on the basis of a different econometric analysis that:

> It is a mistake to blame these economic troubles on the troubles. Indeed it could be argued that while the troubles have led to a loss of manufacturing jobs their net effect on the regional economy has been positive, due to the induced expansion of public-sector expenditure and employment.[25]

Political violence must be a factor in, say, the decisionmaking on investment location at a transnational headquarters, but only one factor amongst many. Nor can we easily disentangle the relative causation or weight of political violence, government policy and international economic factors in relation to unemployment. Without wishing to minimize the impact of the troubles we can only say that it is not the sole or even the main issue in relation to the economic decline of the North in the 1970s.

International capitalism had exhausted the upswing of the long postwar boom by around 1969. A downswing or depressive phase of the long waves of capitalist development now began. As in the South of Ireland, the recessions of 1973 and 1979 were to have a severe impact in Northern Ireland.

This impact was, moreover, accentuated by the already over-dependent and over-specialized nature of the local economy. Continuing our coverage of the three sectors of production we note in Table 3.4 how the manufacturing sector shrunk in the 1970s and 1980s.

Table 3.4: Sectoral Employment, 1971–91 (%)

	1971	1981	1991
Agriculture	11	8	7
Industry	42	30	25
Services	47	62	68

Source: Northern Ireland Annual Abstract of Statistics.

So we find agriculture's terminal decline stabilizing, a once predominantly industrial economy shrinking dramatically and a massive two-thirds of the active population engaged in the service sector. Another way of looking at this industrial crisis is to note that by the mid 1980s the number of people unemployed had actually outstripped the number still employed in manufacturing. The once proud outpost of Britain's Industrial Revolution was no longer.

An obvious repercussion of the international recession was to be a decline of foreign investment in the North of Ireland. To the economic planners who had pinned their hopes on the transnational corporations as the motor of economic growth this was to be a severe blow. During an earlier phase, the transnationals seemed part of a virtuous circle of investment, linkages and development. But in the 1970s a vicious circle of disinvestment, inflation, unemployment and de-industrialization set in. Whereas between 1966 and 1971 foreign investment led to the opening of 51 factories and the creation of 11,600 jobs, between 1972 and 1976, there were only 15 new openings and 900 jobs created. Later we note that whereas in 1981 foreign companies accounted for 23 per cent of industrial employment, by 1986 this proportion had shrunk to 16 per cent. Even these bare figures of decline mask the full picture, because in the 1970s foreign capital tended to operate by acquiring existing enterprises hit by crisis. These were usually small firms compared to the large 500 or more employee firms of the 1960s. As Paul Teague notes, 'The acquisition method of entry generates only minor positive spin-offs for the host country in terms of employment creation and capital expenditure.'[26] Meanwhile the South of Ireland seemed able to continue to attract foreign investment which only accentuated the 'catching up' compared to the North.

At this stage we can explore the sectoral breakdown outlined above in more detail, starting with manufacturing. This sector has declined continuously throughout the 1970s and 1980s, with employment in 1985 having dropped by nearly half compared to the early 1970s. Some sub-sectors collapsed almost completely, such as artificial fibres which was once the star performer. Plastics and metal goods had a similar, if not quite so dramatic, negative fate. On the other hand some sectors such as aircraft (Shorts) and motor vehicles (despite the spectacular De Lorean failure) have done better.

In Table 3.5 we can see the dramatic decline in manufacturing employment since 1970, which contrasts with a slight rise in manufacturing output due to increased labour productivity caused by the rationalization of production during this period.

Table 3.5: Manufacturing Employment and Output, 1970–90

	Manufacturing employment	Manufacturing output Index (1985:100)
1970	180,600	105
1975	159,200	110
1980	136,000	102
1985	108,000	100
1990	105,000	113
1970–90	–42%	+7.6%

As to the service sector, it clearly cannot be divorced from the political context. To deal with the renewed struggle for national liberation in the 1970s, the state was forced to increase its security spending. Thus public administration and defence employees (which do not include the armed forces other than the Ulster Defence Regiment) increased from 47,000 to 59,000 between 1974 and 1985. Thousands of jobs were created by expansion of the police force, the prison service and the 'security industry' generally. In terms of social services there was also an expansion in employment, although to a considerable extent this was a matter of Northern Ireland 'catching up' with the UK. Under the rubric of health and education we find employment increasing from 78,000 in 1974 to 106,000 in 1985. It was this massive increase in service employment which partly compensated for de-industrialization during this period. We should bear in mind, however, that much of this employment was part-time. Whereas in 1971, 10 per cent of workers were in part-time employment, this percentage had risen to 23 per cent by 1987. It should be noted that fully 38 per cent of women workers in 1987 were in part-time jobs (see also Chapter 4) overall, so the expansion of the service sector cannot be seen as a durable base for economic development.

As a result of the decline of foreign investment during this period, the government began to turn increasingly to local small businesses as a possible saviour of the situation. Between 1972 and 1983 the Industrial Development Board (IDB) and its predecessors promoted 57,000 jobs, and the Local Economic Development Unit (LEDU) a further 15,334. By 1987, the IDB and LEDU were promoting a similar amount of jobs – approximately 4,000 each. The LEDU strategy dovetails with the British government's turn towards supply-side economics and the creation of an 'enterprise culture'. However, if the big prestige projects, such as De Lorean, guided by the IDB could collapse, the small-business orientation of LEDU also had its limitations. A study by Hamilton concluded that of the 23,000 jobs promoted by the IDB and LEDU between 1982 and 1988, only 40 per cent were in place by the end of the period.[27] In conclusion, the net effect of employment creation by assisted firms cannot be considered sufficient to reverse the crisis. One should also bear in mind that each IDB promoted job actually costs over £25,000, alongside which LEDU's average of around £6,000 seems cheap, but neither can be a viable strategy for sustained economic growth.

In terms of causes of the economic crisis we have mentioned the international context and the particular historical background. Government policies also, of course, can be seen to contribute to the debacle. Under British Labour Party rule in the mid 1970s, Northern Ireland received a substantial increase in public expenditure. When the economic regime of 'Thatcherism' began in 1979, Northern Ireland began to experience the harsh reality of monetarism and later supply-side economics (although some economists argue that Northern Ireland was sheltered from some of its worst effects for political reasons). Parity with the UK had once meant that Northern Ireland got health and social services 'beyond its means', but now parity meant harsh cutbacks. As O'Dowd and co-authors note: 'Although Labour Direct Rule presided over a rapidly declining industrial base, the fully fledged Tory policy of "making Britain competitive" has even more disastrous implications for the local [NI] economy.'[28] This accelerated decline is well captured by these authors' reminder that while the linen industry lasted for 200 years, the synthetic fibres industry collapsed after 20 years, but De Lorean was only open for 2 years. To some extent 'Thatcherism' was faced by political constraints in Northern Ireland and the hard-faced attitude towards 'lame ducks' could not be applied quite so ruthlessly to key employers such as the shipyard. Nevertheless, the decade of 'Thatcherism' in the North of Ireland undoubtedly hastened and deepened the economic crisis.

Bob Rowthorn and Naomi Wayne in a striking metaphor refer to Northern Ireland as a 'workhouse economy' where those who are not unemployed are mainly engaged in servicing and controlling each other.[29] Though perhaps exaggerated, and certainly unflattering, the analogy is basically valid. It is now relatively few people who are engaged in the production of tradeable goods or services. Most of those remaining in employment are either engaged in repression, providing for social reproduction (health and education) or are selling goods. If Northern Ireland began life as a contributor to Britain's imperial coffers, it was by the 1980s being subsidized to the tune of £1,700 million per annum by the itself ailing ex-imperial power. Like the workhouses of old, it is taxes levied on an external population which alone can finance the growing gap between imports and exports. What came together in the 1980s was a catastrophic combination of international factors, monetarist-oriented governments and the long-term decline of a small peripheral economy divorced from its natural hinterland – the rest of Ireland. Different aspects of that crisis will now be examined in more detail.

The current crisis

The economic crisis of the North is far more severe and structural than that of the South. Economists are loath to view any crisis as terminal, but Northern Ireland does seem to be reaching the end of the road as a

viable economic entity. This, of course, is not unrelated to its status as
a failed political entity, but we shall try to confine ourselves here to the
economic aspect. Even after a halting recovery from the 1979–82
recession, the Northern Irish economy continued to face serious
problems as the Northern Ireland Economic Council (NIEC) recognized: 'The underlying negative feature has been and is the weakness
of the manufacturing sector as a whole . . . [and] the virtually static
levels of real public expenditure in the Province.'[30] A partial recovery
of the clothing industry and a certain expansion of the private services
sector cannot compensate for these underlying trends. In another report
the NIEC states that: 'In the medium to long-term basic demographic
factors allied to the difficulties posed by peripherality present major
challenges for the economy.'[31] The demographic factors referred to are
the steady increase in the working population which is not halted by an
increase in outward migration (see Chapter 7). Overall then we have a
peripheral regional economy now de-industrializing and increasingly
dependent on state expenditure. The prospect of operating within a
unified European market can only be daunting.

In 1982, James Prior, then Secretary of State for Northern Ireland,
referred to the shipyard Harland and Wolf as 'the symbol of industrial
Belfast'. Yet this symbol of the Industrial Revolution and bastion of the
Protestant labour aristocracy was by then a mere shadow of its former
self. Whereas in the mid 1950s it still employed around 22,000 workers,
by the mid 1980s there were less than 4,000 working in the yard. Even
'slimmed down' it was not proving profitable and received by the late
1980s some £15,000 per annum in government subsidies. By the mid
1980s it was, however, being targeted for 'privatization' as part of the
Tory drive to denationalize. The government agreed to write off the
existing debt of H & W, and provided loan stock of £60m and grant
assistance of £38.7m to the new company. A management–employee
buyout was eventually accepted. For the aircraft company, Shorts, a
similar deal was made with the Canadian company Bombardier. The
NIEC comments on both operations that: 'It is difficult not to conclude
therefore that while privatization may offer greater opportunities for
business initiative free from the restraints of government inertia it will
certainly increase the risks to employment substantially.'[32] Thus, for
example, while Shorts employs only 7,000 people directly, it supports
indirectly another 3,000 jobs and provides an important skill base for
the local economy, so, as NIEC note: 'Any loss of employment in the
company would therefore be a serious blow to the local economy.'[33]

If the decline of the shipyard is a symbol of Protestant Belfast so West Belfast is a symbol of Catholics in the North of Ireland. A comprehensive survey of the area has recently been carried out by Obair, the West Belfast Unemployment Campaign, whose overall conclusion is that:

> By the onset of the current recession, almost three-quarters of the jobs on which the area depended had disappeared. Attempts to broaden the North's narrow and declining industrial base largely by-passed West Belfast and, but for the expansion of public sector employment associated with the growth of the welfare state, the area would have become an economic wasteland.[34]

With unemployment rates well in excess of 50 per cent that judgement seems practically generous. In the second half of the 1970s a few industrial firms – including the notorious De Lorean – had been established in the area but this investment proved to be volatile. Now, largely part-time or casual employment in health, education and the building sectors hardly fills the gaps left by long-term decline and structural discrimination. Pointing to the IRA campaign as the cause of this crisis is hardly credible. Even isolating political violence as a cause of economic decline, we would have to seek its cause in the political failure of the Northern Ireland state and the ongoing discrimination against the nationalist minority.

What Northern Ireland was suffering by the mid 1980s was a 'jobs crisis' of massive proportions. Historically, the North had always had a relatively high level of long-term unemployment. By the mid 1980s, when unemployment had nearly reached 20 per cent, over half of these were classed as long-term unemployed, that is to say they had been out of work for over a year. Of course, these figures hide regional variations and some areas suffer from much higher rates of unemployment. Our point here, however, relates to the overall problems of the economy and its seeming inability to offer reasonable job prospects in the future. A study of the IDB's job-creation schemes by the NIEC concludes in this respect 'that unless it was to achieve a rate of jobs creation far in excess of its past performance, the IDB is unlikely to have a significant impact on the overall level of unemployment in the Province'.[35] Compared to the continuing high levels of unemployment, the achievements of the IDB 'would appear to be negligible' according to this government report. So, we can conclude that employment in the North will at best remain static. Even if the British economy enters a sustained upswing – itself highly doubtful – the Northern Irish periphery is unlikely to match that recovery, at least based on present trends.

Some economists have posed a reactionary solution to the 'jobs crisis'. Extending British conservative economic ideology to Ireland it was easy to discern that Northern workers were 'pricing themselves out of a job' by expecting wages and conditions similar to those in Britain. If wages fell, firms would become more competitive, exports would increase, new firms would be attracted and the virtuous circle of economic growth would be resumed. However attractive in terms of neo-classical economics, Cambridge economists David Canning and colleagues conclude that: 'For theoretical and practical reasons wage-cutting does not provide a viable economic development programme for Northern Ireland.'[36] Skilled staff faced by a wage reduction would simply migrate. If unemployment benefit was cut, the unskilled wage would drop, but these workers could simply move to Britain. This would merely represent a geographical displacement of unemployment. In practice the low wages in Northern Ireland in the 1950s – up to a third lower than those in Britain – did not lead to a massive inflow of capital. In fact, increased emigration will be encouraged and there are signs that this may become a major element in the government's economic strategy. Then we would be back to the classical age of imperialism when Ireland provided a reservoir of labour-power for Britain's Industrial Revolution.

By far the post popular culprit for the 'jobs crisis' is, of course, the ongoing campaign of the IRA. We have already noted at the start of the last section that the relative economic impact of political violence is probably not that great. Economist Norman Gibson, in trying to quantify the impact of the political crisis on the economy concludes that 'both unemployment and the growth of the economy as measured by conventionally defined GDP data may in actuality have been little different from what they would have been if there had been no crisis'.[37] Certainly the local economy has been distorted by the troubles in ways which might affect its subsequent potential. Yet the 10,000 jobs 'lost' through the troubles (by reduction of inward investment in the main) would if restored make little impact on the overall situation. The fact is that the political violence is a structural result of partition and not just an artificial excrescence which could be shut off as one does a tap. For that matter we could calculate the number of potential jobs through increased linkages which could have resulted from partition not occurring. Ultimately all of these exercises are somewhat artificial. The point here is simply that political violence cannot be seen as the determinant cause of Northern Ireland's economic decline.

The real reasons for the seemingly terminal decline of Northern

Ireland's economy have already been mentioned in the course of this chapter. The underlying causes are, of course, historical and relate to the way the North of Ireland was incorporated into the international capitalist division of labour in the nineteenth century. Dependence on exports to Britain and a distorted over-specialized industrial structure set the parameters of the North's development. Britain's own decline since around the First World War took the North of Ireland with it and left it particularly vulnerable to the external economic shocks of the 1970s. The gradual decline of local capitalist enterprises since the Second World War appeared to be compensated for by the transnational companies. These, however, operated through 'branch plants' which neither created linkages with the local economy nor provided a secure durable pattern of development. In the most recent phase of economic decline state dependency has become the main form of dependency. For 1990–2 the British government has allocated £684m for law and order, £460m for the police authority and £124m to the prison service. These now appear to be the only growth industries and a sombre reminder of everyday life in the North.

Having started this section asserting that we would concentrate on the economic aspects of the crisis, it might be permissable now, at the end, to return to politics. We have in Northern Ireland a state carved out of a single political unit, which for 70 years has maintained its 'otherness'. Yet today its distinctiveness is not a more mature regional level of industrialization but its more acute economic and political crisis. For 20 years there has been a sustained, and practically unparalleled, political and military campaign for national reunification. Whatever way is found out of the crisis under present arrangements – and capitalism is infinitely adaptable – there will be no space for a sustained economic recovery or the resources for a generous reformist strategy. Not even the most optimistic scenarios of the British government allow for this option. Even if the IRA campaign eventually subsides – and this is very dubious on present trends – that would not lead to economic recovery. Increasingly, the main beneficiaries of industrialization under Britain auspices – the Protestant working class or at least sections of it – will find themselves out in the cold. From all sides the North's economy will be under threat, be it from the regional rationalization implicit in the 1992 project, an insurgent movement for the final removal of the British presence in Ireland, and even from its once-satisfied beneficiaries.

4

Workers and the Economy

For most economists, workers represent merely a 'factor of production', to be discussed in the same technical terms as the rate of exchange, investment policy or inflation. Yet workers are something more, or rather different, than these economic processes. Workers, quite simply, produce all the wealth of a country. Workers are at the very heart of a capitalist economy and not some peripheral problem to be left to the labour economists. We would also argue that the health, or otherwise, of an economy can be judged by its ability to provide work and a decent living standard to all of a country's inhabitants. On this basis we set out to describe who works where in the Irish economy, the problems of unemployment and migration, and the relationship between gender, religion and employment.

Who works where

Employment structures change with the evolution of an economy. More specifically, the changing patterns of capital accumulation set the parameters for the distribution of labour across an economy. The class structure itself also interacts with capital accumulation, setting limits on what is possible or not. Class conflict also dictates how income distribution is established; it is not simply a technical matter determined by Gross National Product (GNP) or productivity rates. With these reservations in mind we can proceed to analyse the changing patterns of employment in the South.

Until 1961 we note a relative stability in the class structure. The largest group of gainfully employed males was the category of self-employed in agriculture, who in 1961 still accounted for one-third of the total. Agricultural labourers still accounted for 10 per cent of the total in 1961 but henceforth would decline. The urban manual working class rose steadily to account for one-quarter of employment in 1961.

The non-manual employees were slightly less numerous but still important. Overall, we note an occupational structure where self-employment and family property is still of crucial importance.

Consequent on the South's 'economic revolution' of 1959, as the economy shifted from protectionism to export orientation, so the dynamic of capitalist advance began to act on the occupational structure. The proportion of the male labour force in farming was cut in half between 1961 and 1981. On the other hand, male white-collar positions doubled, with skilled manual employment achieving nearly this figure. If we disaggregate the 'relatives assisting' category in farming we find that in 1926 this category represented 27 per cent of the male labour force, by 1951 it was a smaller but still significant 16 per cent, but by 1981 it was a mere 2 per cent. David Rothman and Philip O'Connell comment that 'so intense were the changes that it is easy to overlook their incompleteness'.[1] Indeed, even at the start of the 1980s we note a substantial section of the workforce in residual occupational categories, left behind by industrialization, such as the marginal farmers and unskilled labourers. Yet overall the 20 years following the 1959 turn had resulted in a completely new dynamic of accumulation and class. Late in the day, but very rapidly, the South of Ireland became structured and dominated by the capital/wage-labour relation, rather than small-scale production. The massive strike movements of the late 1960s and early 1970s were not unrelated to these changes of course.

Having established in broad outline who works where, we need to consider 'who gets what' a crude but accurate description of income distribution. The bare statistics of Table 4.2 must be our starting point. What Table 4.2 shows is that in 1980 the top 10 per cent of all households received nearly 30 per cent of all direct or market income. On the other hand, the two bottom deciles only received between them half of one per cent of available income. As an Economic and Social Research Institute (ESRI) study notes: 'That comparison starkly represents the degree of inequality in market income present in Ireland today.'[2] However, we must also take into account the impact of income tax and social insurance on income, from which we derive the second column in Table 4.2 on disposable income. This is a fairly reliable index of real household spending power. For the ESRI, the results show that: 'A more "equitable sharing" of the nation's income was not an empty promise.'[3] The idea is that with the rising tide of economic development all boats will rise, with the state playing a further role in fostering greater

Table 4.1: Percentage Distribution of Gainfully Occupied Males by Social Group, 1926–81

| | Employers and self-employed | | | | Employees – salary/wage earners | | | | | Total | |
| | Agricultural | | Non-agricultural | | Non-manual middle class | | Manual (working class) | | | | |
Year	Employers per cent	Self-empl. and rels. assisting per cent	Employers per cent	Self-empl. and rels. assisting per cent	Professional and managerial per cent	Lower non-manual per cent	Skilled man. (non-farm) per cent	Semi-skilled and unskilled man. (non-farm) per cent	Agricultural: labourers per cent		
1926	4.4	39.1	2.2	5.5	3.7	12.1	6.7	11.7	14.1	950,000	100.0
1936	4.2	36.7	1.9	6.2	4.1	11.7	7.5	13.3	14.0	974,000	100.0
1946	4.1	35.8	2.3	5.0	4.7	12.2	7.7	13.5	14.1	948,000	100.0
1951	3.0	33.9	2.1	5.6	5.2	13.7	10.2	15.3	10.9	931,000	100.0
1961	1.7	32.3	1.5	5.8	7.3	15.4	12.0	14.6	9.3	820,000	100.0
1971	1.2	24.6	1.8	6.1	10.3	17.7	16.5	15.6	6.3	828,000	100.0
1981	1.5	15.9	4.0	4.8	14.9	20.0	21.2	13.8	3.8	885,400	100.0

Source: R. Breen et al., *Understanding Contemporary Ireland*, Macmillan, 1990.

Table 4.2: Income Distribution in the Republic, 1980
(Share of total income (%))

Decile of population	Direct income	Disposable income
Top 10%	29.7	25.7
2	18.3	16.2
3	14.3	13.0
4	11.5	11.0
5	9.5	9.3
6	7.7	7.9
7	5.7	6.6
8	2.8	5.1
9		3.5
Bottom 10%	0.5	1.7

Source: R. Breen et al., *Understanding Contemporary Ireland*, p. 86.

income equality. Yet the disposable income of the top 10 per cent was still a massive one-quarter of the total available and the bottom 10 per cent only increasing its share to a meagre 1.7 per cent. Hardly a massive redistribution of wealth. Another way of looking at it is that the bottom half of the population had the same income (in fact slightly less) than the top 10 per cent. A large-scale survey of poverty conducted recently by the ESRI concludes that there has been a rise in relative poverty in the 1980s.[4] Certainly the 'meaning' of poverty in Ireland has changed since the times of the Great Famine. But using relative criteria – in this case, falling below 50 per cent of average disposable household income – over 20 per cent of the population suffer from poverty. This is hardly a glowing testimony to 70 years of nominal independence and 20 years of a self-proclaimed 'economic miracle'.

Moving on now to Northern Ireland we do not find the same or comparable statistics to those used above, but nevertheless we can explore the changing structure of occupation and income distribution in that part of Ireland. As with the South a major sea-change in

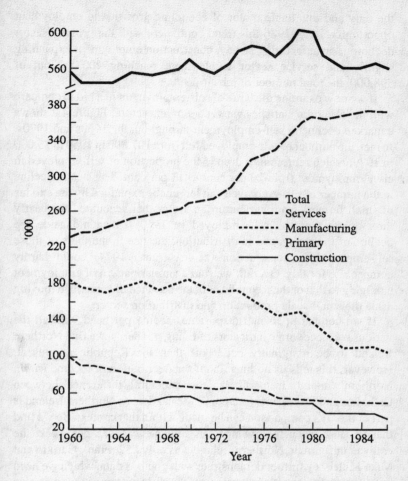

Figure 4.1: Civil Employment, Northern Ireland, 1960–86
Source: NIEC Report 23. *Employment Patterns in Northern Ireland 1950–80*

occupational structure occurred in the course of the 1970s. Figure 4.1 shows the evolution of civil employment by sector between 1960 and 1986.

The overall growth in civil employment masks a decisive shift in its composition. Primary sector employment has fallen steadily, as has manufacturing, except for the odd 'blip'. Employment in the construction industry rose until 1968, but it is the service sector which has been the only and unreliable motor of economic growth and employment opportunity. After 1986 this trend continued, with the primary sector declining, manufacturing steady, construction employment expanding slightly and service sector employment reaching 400,000 out of 598,000, the total number of jobs in 1990.

If we now examine the issue of self-employment in a bid to compare with the Southern statistics we get a similar picture. Figure 4.2 shows a marked decline in self-employment throughout the 1960s and 1970s. In fact, the number of self-employed fell from 107,800 in 1950 to 75,000 in 1979, which represents a drop in the proportion of self-employed in civil employment from 20 per cent to 13 per cent. The steady decline in the number of self-employed can largely be explained by the exodus of small farmers from agriculture, a sector that accounted for nearly three-quarters of the self-employed in 1950. Taken alongside the decline of those engaged in distribution, the rise in numbers of those self-employed in construction (at least until 1974) could hardly compensate for this. Overall, we find a similar pattern of employment emerging to that of the Republic with the advance of capitalism moving aside the small-scale production and distribution sector.

If we compare personal disposable income per head with all the various socioeconomic indicators of living standards, we find Northern Ireland to be marginally better off than the Republic at present. However, this tells us nothing about the distribution of income *within* Northern Ireland, in particular the structural difference between Catholics and Protestants (see pp. 91–97). Also, as Northern Ireland is part of the UK, comparison can be made within that context. So we find that in 1982 when the average UK income was £75 per week, the equivalent figure in Northern Ireland was only £52. Frank Gafikin and Mike Morrissey further demonstrate with copious data, which we need not enumerate, that: 'Information on the distribution of incomes also points to Northern Ireland having a disproportionate concentration in lower income bands.'[5] This is reflected in the level of household expenditure, with Northern Ireland households having only three-quarters of the purchasing power of their British counterparts. Northern Ireland has, in brief, remained a peripheral and disadvantaged appendage to the British economy. The British welfare state has cushioned the decline of living standards for those falling into the 'poverty trap', but nothing points towards a secure economic future for its population. Northern Ireland is no longer a privileged region within Ireland and

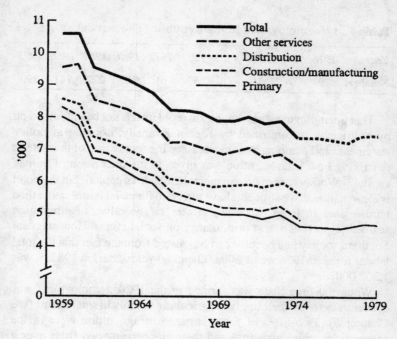

Figure 4.2: Self-employment, 1959–79
Source: DMS Gazette No 3.

uneven development is now working in reverse with the South the developing pole.

Unemployment

According to the Economist Intelligence Unit, unemployment in the South is projected to rise steadily and: 'The resulting figure of 306,000 unemployed by 1992 [in fact the fugure was 278,400] will represent the most serious economic and social problem facing the Irish economy in the 1990s.'[6] This undoubtedly is true, but in terms of establishment politics, the severity of this verdict does not appear to have sunk in. The continuous and massive outflow of workers through migration somehow seemed to remove the urgency of the unemployment question, seen clearly in Table 4.3.

Table 4.3: Unemployment in the Republic (Thousands)

Year	1926	1936	1946	1951	1961	1971	1981	1986	1988	1993
Numbers	79	86	64	45	59	61	126	227	241	299

That unemployment as a long-term problem has not been focused on by politicians is confirmed by Kieran Kennedy:'Looking at policy statements and planning documents since the foundation of the state, it is striking how little attention was given to the dimension of human capital.'[7] Workers are of course more than 'human capital' but the point is clear: nationalist politicians have turned to financial issues rather than human ones in large part because the 'safety valve' of emigration seemed to prevent unrest or militancy on social issues. How stagnant Southern society had become can be gauged from the fact that the total labour force in 1926 was 1,300,000 and 60 years later, in 1986, it was 1,302,000.

When the Free State was formed in the 1920s, employment was concentrated overwhelmingly in agriculture, mainly in small farms (see Chapter 5). Two-fifths of those engaged in agriculture were in the category 'relatives assisting' and their number dropped from over a quarter of a million in the 1920s to barely 24,000 in 1980. Thus, we can assume that there was considerable disguised unemployment in agriculture to start off with. Decline in employment in this area meant that other areas had to increase dramatically to absorb the surplus, let alone create an increase in employment. This is, of course, par for the course in most post-independence states striving for economic development. Nevertheless, as Kennedy notes, 'The structure that existed in the new Irish state, cut off from its industrial arm in the north-east, was particularly daunting from the viewpoint of raising employment.'[8] The low technological level which the South found itself in created the scope for technological advance which, though essential, did not necessarily provide employment. Thus, labour productivity (in the form of GDP per worker) rose by 2.5 per cent between 1926 and 1986, but employment actually dropped by 0.2 per cent. The 2.3 per cent growth in GDP volume achieved in these 60 years did not represent a sufficiently high growth of output to have an impact on employment. This is the necessary structural context to understand how deeprooted unemployment is today.

The unemployment rate during the 1970s oscillated around the 5–6 per cent mark, but after reaching 10 per cent in 1982, rose to 16–17 per cent for the rest of the decade. Just as significant, the proportion of long-term (more than one year) unemployed rose from 15 per cent in the early 1970s to nearly 50 per cent by the end of the 1980s. Before the 1960s we must recall the high proportion of the population who were classed as 'self-employed' both on the land and in the cities. This sector could not, therefore, become officially 'unemployed'. Another illusion is due to the high rates of emigration which kept unemployment rates low at home only by exporting the problem. In more recent decades, the proletarianization of the population –more and more people becoming directly subsumed by the capital/wage labour relation –has meant that unemployment rates became a more realistic reflection of the situation. Richard Breen et al. write that:

> Also striking is the degree to which unemployment has been concentrated in the working classes: the level of unemployment among non-agricultural unskilled workers fell below 25 per cent at only one census, while that for the service class only once exceeded three per cent.[9]

This is perhaps not surprising for a capitalist society but it belies the popular image presented by Fianna Fail whose main social base – the urban and rural less well-off sectors – were precisely the main victims of unemployment and the emigrant ship.

As a recent ESRI survey on poverty in the South concludes: 'Unemployment is the single most important cause of poverty in Ireland, as our results demonstrate.'[10] The ESRI data shows that the risk of poverty for households headed by an unemployed person was between 2.5 and 5.5 times the average risk depending where the 'poverty line' was drawn. The rise in the overall unemployment rate from 8 per cent in 1980 to 18 per cent in 1987 was thus matched by an increase in poverty. And that in a state which already had a higher proportion of the population below the relative poverty line than most European countries, including Britain. Furthermore, relative poverty is not only higher in Ireland than in Britain, but living standards are of course lower. While considerable economic growth was achieved in the 1970s this was not reflected in lower unemployment rates. Conversely, the impact of stagnation in the 1980s was decisive in creating more unemployment and thus poverty. Dealing with unemployment would not only free up resources which could then be deployed productively, but it would also play a significant role in alleviating poverty. To date, there is little sign that political leaders or establishment economists have taken the issues sufficiently seriously. In the meantime, unemployment is set to rise in the 1990s, both in absolute and relative terms.

Since its inception, the state of Northern Ireland has always had a considerably higher rate than that of Britain as we can see in Table 4.4.

Table 4.4: Unemployment Rates, Northern Ireland and Britain, 1923–90 (%)

	1923	1926	1929	1932	1935	1938	1947
N. Ireland	18.2	23.2	14.8	27.2	24.8	28.3	7.9
G. Britain	11.7	12.5	10.4	22.1	15.5	12.9	2.0
	1953	1968	1974	1979	1983	1989	1990
N. Ireland	10.9	7.1	5.7	12.1	21.0	15.7	13.4
G. Britain	2.2	2.4	2.6	6.6	10.4	6.9	5.6

We note that only in 1947, 1968 and 1974 did the Northern Irish rate drop below two figures, and even then that percentage is two or three times that of Britain. In 1953, when British politicians were saying that all was for the best in the best of all possible worlds, the North of Ireland was suffering a *five times* greater unemployment rate. Looking at the long-term trend of unemployment since the 1920s we note the steady rise to nearly 30 per cent into the 1930s and the slump. During the Second World War unemployment actually dropped to 3.4 per cent in 1944 but in the postwar period of 'full employment' in Britain, the North's unemployment rate hovered around 10 per cent. Though the early 1970s saw a recovery, unemployment again began to rise in the late 1970s and early 1980s to top 20 per cent. A fragile economic recovery in the late 1980s led to a decline in unemployment to 16 per cent, although there is considerable debate on the reliability of this data and, in particular, the extent to which the government gradually removes more and more people from the unemployment register.

A graphic representation of the rise of unemployment in the 1970s and early 1980s can be gained from Figure 4.3. A decline in

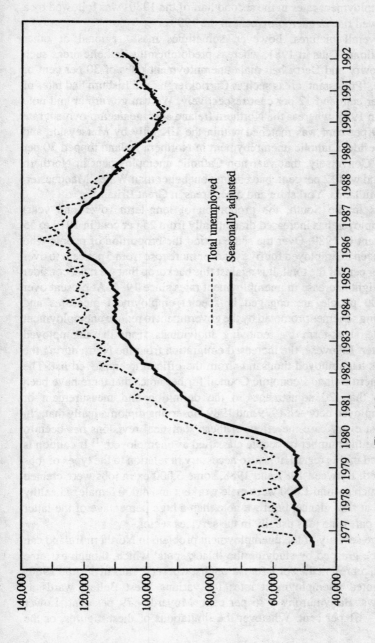

Figure 4.3: Unemployment in Northern Ireland, 1973–92
Source: Department of Economic Development press notice – Unemployment August 1992

unemployment rates in the second half of the 1980s was followed by a renewed rise in unemployment in the 1990s.

Overall pictures, however, sometimes mask regional or other variations. Thus in 1981, whereas predominantly Catholic areas such as Newry and Derry had male unemployment rates of 30 per cent or more, 'Protestant' areas such as Carrickfergus and Lisburn had rates of 16 per cent and 12 per cent respectively. We can go further and note that in 1985, whereas the Northern Ireland average unemployment rate of 19 per cent was matched within the UK only by Merseyside and Clydeside, Catholic unemployment in Northern Ireland topped 30 per cent. Conversely, that year non-Catholic unemployment in Northern Ireland was 12 per cent, bad enough but better than Wales, Manchester, the Midlands, Yorkshire and other areas in Great Britain.

As in the South, the proportion of long-term (over one year) unemployed has increased dramatically from 25 per cent in 1979 to 55 per cent in 1989. Over the same period the proportion of people who had been unemployed for five years or more rose from 5 per cent to over 15 per cent of the total. It is against this backdrop that we must consider the slight decrease in unemployment rates since 1986. At present over 33,000 people are engaged in special employment measures and training schemes promoted by the government to reduce unemployment in the short-term by removing individuals from the unemployed register. Likewise, the increased emigration from the North during the 1980s has removed thousands from the official unemployed list. The Northern Ireland Economic Council further notes that there have been more than 20 adjustments to the definition and measurement of unemployed between 1979 and 1989, observing diplomatically that: 'In almost every case the effect of these statistical revisions has been to reduce the number of people classified as unemployed.'[11] If caution is needed in this regard, it is also necessary in relation to the types of jobs created. Between 1987 and 1988, some 5,000 extra jobs were created of which around 1,000 were male workers and 4,000 female, a healthy trend at first glance, until we note than a high percentage of the latter were part-time jobs usually in the services sector.

The severity of the unemployment problem in Northern Ireland can best be grasped by studying the 'black spots' which, though extreme cases, represent the norm for nationalist workers. Thus in the mid 1980s we noted unemployment rates for various West Belfast wards as follows: Ballymurphy – 86 per cent, Moyard – 79 per cent, Lower Falls – 61 per cent. Whatever the limitations of these figures, or the

importance of the 'black economy' in those areas, they do give an idea
of the level of work deprivation present. In fact, as the West Belfast
unemployment campaign notes, 'The severity of the situation is perhaps
better illustrated by considering *employment* rather than unemployment
rates.'[12] Thus in the mid 1980s Northern Ireland's unemployment rate
of 14–20 per cent was matched by the *employment* rates of Ballymurphy (14 per cent) and Moyard (20 per cent). As a survey of
unemployment by area concludes, 'The very high rates of unemployment throughout West Belfast, are associated with a wide range of
personal consequences from depression to suicide, from heart disease
to premature death.'[13] It is not surprising that some have referred to
unemployment as the North's 'other crisis'. But it is a crisis closely
related to the failure of partition and, in particular, the terminal decline
of the six-county economy. It is not thus 'another' crisis but part and
parcel of the crisis of colonial rule in Ireland.

Workers and emigration

Emigration only occurs because of the absolute or relative failure of a
particular economic system to provide a livelihood for all its population.
A declining workforce is truly a sign of a failed economic system. In
Table 4.5 we compare the workforces of Britain and Ireland from 1841
to the 1970s.

Table 4.5: Workforce of Britain and Ireland: 1841, 1911, 1970s

Period	*Britain*	*Ireland*		
		26 Cos	*6 Cos*	*Total*
1841	7,094	2,715	797	3,512
1911	17,758	1,274	543	1,817
1970–80 (average)	25,235	1,156	602	1,758

Source: R. Crotty, *Ireland in Crisis*, 1986, p. 2.

With a broad historical sweep Table 4.5 shows to what extent
Ireland's capacity to sustain its labour force has fallen behind that of
Britain. In 1841, Ireland had a workforce half the size of that of Britain,
but by the 1970s this proportion has fallen to barely 7 per cent. The

North of Ireland shows a less precipitous decline and, in fact, a small increase between 1911 and the 1970s. Overall, however, both parts have been a failure in terms of securing a livelihood for their people. If emigration has provided a 'safety valve' for the tensions which would otherwise have erupted, it has also led to the loss of some of the country's most motivated workers.

Sir William Wilde in 1864 described those left behind after the big post-Famine wave of emigration as 'the poor, the weak, the old, the lame, the sick, the blind, the dumb, and the imbecile and insane'. We need not accept this characterization to recognize that emigration sapped the life blood of the Irish people. From 1800 to 1920 over 8 million men, women and children left Ireland, which represented a figure equivalent to the population of the country at its peak, just before the Great Famine. Heavy and prolonged emigration could only hinder the prospects of economic development in Ireland. David Fitzpatrick argues that: 'A further effect of continuous depopulation was to reduce post-Famine Ireland's attractiveness as a field for investment, and so to make still more improbable the diffusion of industrial and urban expansion throughout Ireland.'[14] Clearly depopulation could not prevent industrialization – witness Ulster's nineteenth century expansion – but the ever-shrinking Irish market was most certainly a disincentive to investment. Emigration thus played a crucial role in retarding both agricultural and industrial modernization in Ireland. Those who remained in Ireland after the Famine were thus faced with a continuation of the traditional forms of exploitation. Emigration once commenced was also, of course, self-perpetuating as those abroad helped 'pull' more people away from Ireland.

If Ireland under the Act of Union was a place most of its people wanted to leave, what was the situation in that part of Ireland which set about independence after 1920? Table 4.6 sets out the bare figures of emigration from the 26 counties. If we take a broad overview we find that between 1926 and 1986, 17,200 people per annum left the South of Ireland, never to return. This, however, includes the anomalous 1970s during which, for the first time in the state's history, the flow of migration was actually reversed and some 13,000 people per annum returned home. Overall, however, and particularly on recent trends we have a picture of an economy which has failed to deliver a livelihood for its people.

The Republic's government did make one attempt to seriously address the problem of emigration when it set up the Emigration

Table 4.6: Net Emigration from the South, 1926–86

Period	Net emigration	Net emigration per annum
1926–36	166,751	16,675
1936–46	187,111	18,711
1946–51	119,568	23,914
1951–6	196,763	39,353
1956–61	212,003	42,401
1961–6	80,605	16,121
1966–71	53,906	10,781
1971–9	–108,934	–13,617
1979–81	5,045	2,523
1981–6	75,300	15,060
1986–90	178,000	35,600

Source: R. Breen et al., *Understanding Contemporary Ireland*, p.147.

Commission in 1948 with the brief of formulating a national population policy. That this was a major concern is not surprising when we consider that it was an axiom of Irish nationalism that the population would grow rapidly following independence. When the Emigration Commission reported in 1954 it argued that: 'A steadily increasing population should occupy a high place among the criteria by which the success of national policy should be judged.'[15] Yet the Commission seemed to stress the short-term financial benefits of emigration, with one member arguing somewhat cynically, though no doubt realistically, that emigration 'released social tensions which would otherwise explode and made possible a stability of manners and customs which would otherwise be the subject of radical change'.[16] In practice, the Commission did not suggest any measures to stem emigration beyond a pious hope that improved social and economic conditions might make it unnecessary. This conclusion seemed to belie the stress the Commission laid on the urgency of the emigration problem. In retrospect, though, it is perhaps even more striking that this was the only major initiative taken by the new Irish state in relation to an ongoing bleeding away of its population.

Following from the census data of Table 4.6, we note that net migration increase dramatically in 1985 to reach 20,000, in 1986 it reached 28,000, and in 1989 the figure was 42,000. These figures compare with those of the postwar period when emigration picked up dramatically. Most observers agree that this is a different type of emigration, however, characterized by much higher levels of education and skills. The Economist Intelligence Unit noted recently: 'The "brain drain" implicit in the most recent emigration of skilled and educated workers has been a subject of controversy and raises questions regarding the levels of public expenditure on education, particularly at tertiary level.'[17] It would seem to be implied that perhaps the state should not waste money training graduates if these are going to take their skills elsewhere. It should perhaps be asked why 27 per cent of those with higher degrees emigrated in 1985. Certainly, the advantages of a skilled, educated, relatively cheap and quite pliable workforce have been well advertised by the IDA. What happens, of course, is that individuals may prefer to exercise their skills where they will be better paid. The advent of the single economic market in Europe can only be expected to accentuate this trend, as a new skilled and mobile white-collar worker takes advantage of the new and wider economic environment.

The Economist Intelligence Unit paints a picture of continuing emigration at a rate of 25,000 per annum, 'though this might increase given the employment outlook'; an unemployment figure of over 300,000 by 1992, and a growing section of the population marginalized from mainstream economic life. However, this international capitalist organ does not despair, because this bleak social scenario 'is not expected to lead to significant social unrest in the medium term, due both to the safety valve of emigration and the general weakness of the political opposition'.[18] Indeed, while opinion surveys regularly show emigration as an issue near the top of the agenda for ordinary people in the South, in terms of the mainstream political agenda it does not appear too prominent. A short-sighted attitude by the trade unions could also be expected to lead to no more than ritual denouncing of emigration. If there are 25,000 less workers on the labour market each year there are 25,000 less jobs that need to be created, or so we are led to think. Where the Economist really scores is in locating the weakness of the political opposition in the South to any schemes to restructure capital on the backs of a decomposition of the working class through unemployment and emigration. In this context we can expect emigration to continue to act as a 'safety valve' as it has historically and retard the organic socioeconomic development of the South.

As to Northern Ireland, statistics are harder to come by regarding emigration but the issue is, nevertheless, just as important. John Simpson provides a good attempt to quantify emigration in the North, shown in Table 4.7.

Table 4.7: Net Emigration Rates in Northern Ireland (Rate per 1,000 per annum)

Period	Catholics	Non-Catholics	Total	Republic
1937–51	6.5	2.3	3.7	6.9
1951–61	10.8	4.6	6.7	13.8
1961–71	6.9	2.8	4.3	4.8
1971–81	N/A	N/A	7.2	–3.2
1981–91	N/A	N/A	4.5	14.0

Source: to 1971 J. Simpson, 'Economic Development: Cause or Effect of the Northern Ireland Conflict', in J. Darby (ed.) *Northern Ireland. The Background to the Conflict*, Belfast, Appletree Press, 1983, p. 102. Post 1971 data for the Republic from NESC Report 90 and for Northern Ireland from Northern Ireland Census 1991.

Until the 1960s we note that the North had a net emigration rate around half that of the Republic, although in the 1960s the rates became very similar. We also note that Catholic emigration rates were always around double those for non-Catholics, which, of course, relates to their differential position in the labour market (see pp.91–97). A small point, but perhaps significant in the long run, is the fact that Catholic emigration from the North was actually higher in the 1960s than the overall rate for the Republic. Though the North escaped the massive outflow of the 1950s, it would seem that there has since been a catching up, with Catholics leading the deprivation stakes.

This idea is borne out by the experience of the 1970s during which there was a net out-migration of 100,000 from Northern Ireland, which represents a rate of approximately 7 per 1,000 per annum, and thus a big increase on the previous decade. Demographer Paul Compton concludes that: 'In the absence of any rise in the demand for labour outside Northern Ireland, the present rate of net outflow of 6 to 8,000 per annum may be expected to continue.'[19] Clearly without this 'safety valve', unemployment rates would have increased to something in the order of 30 per cent. There is certainly little likelihood of the Northern Ireland economy itself picking up to the extent that it could stem this flow. As with the South, today's migrant is not the unskilled labourer who went to build Britain's railroads and motorways. As Compton notes, 'the outflow is likely to contain a substantial proportion of highly motivated as well as skilled individuals, i.e. the very people that will be needed at home, if the Northern Ireland economy is to be revived'.[20] Though specific data is not provided it would appear that in recent years Protestant out-migration has become increasingly important, a fact of not only economic but also political significance. Sections of what was once the Protestant 'labour aristocracy' now appear to be reassessing the prospects of their Province.

Women and work

Economists often seem to forget that the working class has two sexes. This is even reflected in the statistics readily available on the labour force, such as those used in the above sections. It is now necessary for us to break down the overall figures and examine the particular role of women workers within the overall picture. In the Republic women have historically had a low participation rate in the labour market. This began to change in the 1970s: whereas in 1971 only 7 per cent of married women were engaged in paid employment, by 1981 this proportion had risen to over 17 per cent. This is undoubtedly related to the dominant patriarchal ethos of Irish society. So much so, that a survey in 1983 found that only one-third of married women wished to return to paid employment, with their main priorities centred around household and child-rearing roles.[21] This compares unfavourably with Britain and most other European states. Nevertheless, the 1970s were a period of profound social change in Ireland, with legislation aimed at ensuring equality of treatment in the labour market for women and the equally essential, improved maternity leave agreements.

By 1987 women represented 32 per cent of the labour force. Another way of looking at this change is to note that whereas in the 1970s only 1 in 13 women were engaged in paid work, by the mid 1980s this proportion had risen to 1 in 5. Younger married women in particular were staying on in the labour market. Table 4.8 shows the sectors in which women were working in 1988.

Table 4.8: Female Employment by Industrial Sector, 1988

Sector	Proportion of women (%)
Agriculture	7.1
Mining	6.2
Manufacturing	29.3
(Textiles, clothing, footwear)	(61.0)
Electricity, Gas and Water	10.9
Building	2.4
Commerce	35.1
Insurance, Finance and Business Services	45.9
Transport, Communication and Storage	19.4
Public Administration and Defence	29.0
Professional Services	59.9
Personal Services	62.3
Other Industries	33.2
TOTAL	32.1

Source: J. Blackwell, *Women in the Labour Force*, Dublin Employment Equality Agency, 1990, p. 7.

We note that women represent more than half the total labour force in professional and personal services, and within the textiles sub-branch of manufacturing. Women also represent nearly half of the labour force in commerce and financial services. On the other hand, women are under-represented in agriculture, mining and building.

During the 1960s, women's earnings were only slightly over half those of men. By 1988 average female weekly earnings were still only 60 per cent those of men, although hourly earnings were slightly higher

at 67 per cent. This is coincidentally the same hourly rate as pertains in
the UK, although women in Denmark earn 86 per cent of the male wage
and women in Italy 85 per cent. As always pay and conditions cannot
be separated from the type of jobs people do. Women are crowded into
a relatively small number of industrial sectors, where low pay prevails.
Thus 75 per cent of clerical workers are women and 65 per cent of textile
and clothing workers are women. Women also tend to be concentrated
more in areas where part-time work prevails. Though there is no
recognized bench-mark for what constitutes part-time work in the
Republic, the number of regular part-time jobs doubled to 6 per cent in
the decade 1977–87. Whereas in 1987 18,000 men were engaged in
part-time work, the number of women so working was 47,000. Though
part-time work does not at present have the overwhelming impact it
does in the North, its role can be expected to increase as employers
across the EC turn to a more casual, more part-time and, often, more
female labour force in the 1990s.

As John Blackwell notes: 'The change in the role of women [in the
Republic] has been one of the most striking features of the past twenty
five years but equally noticeable has been the resistance to changes in
their role.'[22] Before the 1970s, women's place was seen to be firmly in
the home. This was perhaps typified by the marriage bar in the public
services, but there were other professions and skilled occupations where
women were denied entry. Where women did enter the labour market
it was in sexually segregated areas. So much so that in the 1960s a
quarter of women workers were engaged in professions which were 90
per cent or more female in composition. This is the background against
which we must assess the situation in the 1980s. The Anti Discrimination (Pay) Act of 1975 and the Employment Equality Act of 1977 have
undoubtedly had some impact, but the data quoted above puts this in
context. A couple of comparisons may serve to illustrate the limits to
the changing role of women in Ireland. For the female labour force
participation rate in Ireland to reach the EC average, there would have
to be another 90,000+ women workers. To eliminate sex segregation at
work (statistically that is), over 53 per cent of all women would have to
shift to male-dominated occupations. It is significant that neither of
these two changes was any nearer to being achieved in the 1980s.

Northern Ireland has historically had higher female participation
rates in the formal economy than the South. The picture of inequality
is, however, no different and the gender segregation of the labour
market operates just as powerfully. By 1985 women held an all time

high of 46 per cent of all jobs in Northern Ireland. However, we have to note that between 1971 and 1989 the proportion of part-time female jobs doubled from 19 per cent to 39 per cent. Not only are a high proportion of women's jobs part-time but they are also, of course, badly paid. At best women can earn no more than three-quarters of what men in comparable jobs do. In short, as Janet Trewsdale notes: 'Women in both GB and NI are to be found in low status, low paid jobs.'[23] This inequitable sexual division of labour is, of course, inseparable from the patriarchal values and structures which dominate society as a whole. At present we are only analysing the effects of patriarchal capitalism in relation to women and work. We must bear in mind also that if women's role in the formal economy has increased so have female unemployment rates, which climbed nearly fivefold from 2.5 per cent in 1974 to 13 per cent in 1985. In work and out of work, the same as in the home and outside, women are disadvantaged.

In Northern Ireland the 'activity rate' for married females is 45 per cent and for unmarried females 57 per cent. Over 80 per cent of all female employees work in the services sector. Compared to a male rate of 2 per cent, fully 38 per cent of women work part-time. By far the largest number of female part-time workers work in catering, cleaning, hairdressing and similar services. As Janet Trewsdale notes:

> The type of work carried out by women has hardly changed over the decade [to 1987]. The majority of women continue to work in low paid, low status occupations; jobs which, until the cold wind of economic depression blew, would not have been considered by men.[24]

Furthermore, even within occupations we find that women are less likely to hold positions of responsibility and, therefore, better pay. Table 4.9 gives an overall impression of where women in Northern Ireland work and the comparable male proportions. We see that women, especially married women, were represented in the education, welfare and health professions. Women are seriously under-represented in the two managerial categories on the other hand. But, most significant is the fact that half of all women in paid employment are engaged in clerical work and category IX comprising catering, cleaning and hairdressing.

Women's pay should be the same as that of men in comparable occupations according to British and Irish equal pay legislation. However, in 1987 average weekly earnings of manual female workers

Table 4.9: Occupational Analysis: Females by Marital Status and Males, 1985 (%)

	Occupation	Single	Married	Other	Total	Males
		Females				*Males*
I	Managerial and professional and related supporting management and administration	0.5	0.8	0.1	1.3	4.6
II	Professional and related in education, welfare and health	4.3	12.9	0.9	18.1	6.8
III	Literary, artistic and sports	0.2	0.3	0	0.4	0.4
IV	Professional and related in science, engineering and technology	0.2	0.2	0	0.4	4.3
V	Managerial (excluding general management)	1.2	3.4	0.6	5.2	14.2
VI	Clerical and related	9.0	15.0	1.2	25.3	8.4
VII	Selling	3.3	5.3	0.9	9.5	5.0
VIII	Security and protective service	0	0.3	0	0.3	4.0
IX	Catering, cleaning, hairdressing and other professional services	3.4	17.4	3.6	24.5	3.6
X	Farming, fishing and related	0.2	0.3	0	0.5	1.9
XI	Material processing (excluding metal)	3.7	3.5	0.4	7.7	8.5
XII	Processing, making and repairing (metal and electrical)	0.7	0.5	0.1	1.3	14.5
XIII	Painting, repetitive assembling, product inspection etc	1.6	2.0	0	3.6	3.0
XIV	Construction, mining etc	0	0	0	0	6.0
XV	Transport operating, moving and storing materials	0.3	0.1	*	0.5	9.4
XVI	Miscellaneous	0	0.1	0	0.1	2.1
	On government training scheme	1.2	0.1	0	1.3	2.3
	No reply	0	0	0	0	0.7
	TOTALS	29.8	62.2	8.0	100.0	100.0

Note: * Sample size too small to be included

Source: Labour Force Survey, 1985

was 65 per cent that of men. For the non-manual occupations, where women are more numerous, the female average wage was only 60 per cent that of men. So, Equal Pay Acts notwithstanding, women's pay in Northern Ireland lags well behind that of their male counterparts, as well as that of women workers in Britain, of course. It would appear to confirm the hypothesis of a dual labour market with women clustering in certain occupations characterized by low pay. Furthermore, the 1980s have actually seen a widening of pay differentials. This confirms the general impression that in periods of economic recession, sex discrimination and unequal pay are considerably harder to combat. For many male workers one reaction to the hardships of recession is to attack women workers (especially married women) for taking jobs which 'naturally' should go to men. It cannot be expected that the 1984 'equal value' amendment to the 1970 Equal Pay Act will have a major impact on this situation, although a marginal improvement of women's pay should result.

Female unemployment rates are notoriously unreliable. Until the mid 1970s, married women could pay less national insurance but thus not be eligible for unemployment benefit. Now, whereas all are eligible for unemployment benefit, after a year married women are not allowed to claim the follow up supplementary benefit and thus disappear from the official count. Nevertheless, we can note a steady rise in female unemployment rates since the 1970s. It is also useful to study the differential impact of unemployment by region, gender and religion in Table 4.10. We note that though the Northern Ireland average for female unemployment is 5 per cent greater than the British average, for Catholic women the proportion of unemployed is 2.5 times greater.

Workers and religion

If the working class has two sexes, in the North of Ireland it is also divided into two religions – Catholic and Protestant – which constitute two distinct fractions of the working class, with clearly distinguishable roles in the economic structure. It could be argued that the working class in every country is divided according to age, gender, race, religion, region and so on, but it is not always that these differences harden into what is virtually a dual labour market. The dual labour-market model refers to a primary and secondary sector of the labour market: the first

Table 4.10: Unemployment in Northern Ireland and Britain, 1981

	Male (%)	Female (%)
NI Catholics	30.2	17.1
Merseyside	19.5	11.0
NI (Average)	19.1	12.6
Wales	14.8	9.7
Manchester	13.9	8.8
NI (Non-Catholics)	12.4	9.6
Scotland (Clydeside)	11.6	8.4
West Yorkshire	12.4	7.4
Britain (Average)	11.3	7.4
East Anglia	8.5	5.7
Outer metropolitan area	6.6	4.6

Source: B. Rowthorn and N. Wayne, *Northern Ireland. The Political Economy of Conflict*, p. 45.

offers stable, well-paid employment and is a dynamic sector of the economy, the latter offers only low-paid, perhaps part-time work and is centred on low-productivity areas. Trade unions are strong in the primary sector, weak or non-existent in the secondary sector. The model has been applied most successfully to the racially segregated labour markets of the United States. In the North of Ireland, from the very origins of industrialization we can trace the formation of a dual labour market. Once a segregated labour market has been established – and, of course, the level of segregation is not always total – the need for active discrimination becomes less. It is thus not necessary to prove active discrimination to demonstrate that Northern Ireland's labour market is partially segregated on religious grounds.

The 1911 census allows us to examine the religious breakdown of the various trades in Belfast at the height of the Industrial Revolution. Table 4.11 outlines the situation in selected male occupations for Catholic workers.

Table 4.11: Selected Male Occupations/Industries, Catholic Representation, 1911

Industry	Catholic representation (100 = Equality)
Shipbuilding	33
Iron	68
Printing	66
Linen	108
(Spinning)	(146)
(Weaving)	(74)
Bricklayers	97
Painters	86
Carters	120
Dockers	171
Carpenters	54
Plumbers	51
Labourers	141
Butchers	174
Publicans	346

Source: A.C. Hepburn, 'Work, class and religion in Belfast, 1871–1911', *Irish Economic and Social History*, X, 1983, p. 39.

The picture which emerges is a complex one, but the general pattern is, nevertheless, clear. Catholics are over-represented in certain 'traditional' trades such as publicans and butchers, and in the low-paid, and deemed unskilled, categories of labourer, carter and docker.

The highly paid and skilled shipbuilding trades show a massive Catholic under-representation, only slightly less marked for carpenters, plumbers and the iron trade. If we take linen, where Catholics are more or less equally employed we find that a breakdown shows Catholics over-represented in the less well-paid spinning end of the trade. For women, we find a similar picture. If we take just the religious distribution of female commercial clerks we find that in 1911 against 100 for equality, Catholics attain a ratio of 44 against the 138 scored by Presbyterians.

If we now jump forward by 60 years we can examine the data of the 1971 census, doubly significant because it occurred in the last year of the Stormont administration. The basic conclusion of the Fair Employment Agency in analysing this data is that:

> The industrial profiling of Protestants and Roman Catholics demonstrated major areas of Roman Catholic under-representation, most notably Engineering, the Utilities and Insurance, Banking, Finance and Business Services, and the unhealthy over-dependence of Roman Catholic males in the Construction industry. Extending the industrial profile to consider wages it was observed that there was a tendency for those industries which had the highest weekly manual wage in 1971 to be predominantly Protestant, a tendency which was still marked for women.[25]

Though a professional Catholic middle class certainly can now be detected, the 'modal' Catholic male worker was engaged in unskilled manual work. Within industries Catholics are seen to predominate in the lower grades, whereas Protestants hold a disproportionate amount of higher grades. Thus within the 'Catholic' building trade, Catholics represented 55 per cent of labourers, but only 18 per cent of managers. Even in the non-manual occupations there are marked differences in the perceived status of 'Catholic' and 'Protestant' occupations listed in Table 4.12. If we recall that Catholics then represented around one-third of the population we can see how marked over- and under-representation are in these occupations. The status and, of course, pay of the more 'Catholic' occupations, especially when these are predominantly female (for example, hairdressers and housekeepers), compares dramatically with those which are more 'Protestant' and male (for example, managers and government officials).

Today, over 20 years after Britain prorogued Stormont and established Direct Rule over the North we could expect the old sectarian practices in employment to fade away. Certainly that is how British political managers would portray themselves, as above the 'tribal warfare' of Protestants and Catholics. The data does not support such an optimistic scenario, however. The 1981 census data still showed 43

Table 4.12: 'Catholic and 'Protestant' Occupations, 1971

	% Women	% Catholic
1. 'Catholic' occupations		
Publicans	21	73
Waiters, waitresses	84	50
Hairdressers	76	49
Housekeepers	100	48
Nurses	90	43
Teachers	63	39
2. 'Protestant' occupations		
Company secretaries	15	7
Police	3	10
Chemists	11	11
Engineers	–	11
Managers	6	12
Senior government officials	10	13

Source: E. Aunger, 'Religion and occupational class in Northern Ireland', *Economic and Social Review*, 7/11, 1975, p. 7.

per cent of male Cookstown Catholics unemployed and 39 per cent of Catholics in Strabane. Conversely, male Protestants in Belfast had a much lower, 15 per cent, unemployment rate. For Lisburn we find 8 per cent of Protestant males unemployed but 22 per cent of the town's Catholic males. Osborne and Cormack in a broad review of the 1971 to 1981 changes stress the element of continuity above change.[26] They found a small increase in the representation of Catholics in some positions of authority in the labour market. Yet probing behind the overall figures we find that Catholic progress in professional areas tends to be as nurses rather than doctors, or school teachers rather than higher education lecturers. Surveys of the major universities by the Fair Employment Agency suggest that inequality is deeply rooted. Overall, however, it is the ongoing differentials in terms of unemployment which swings the conclusion towards continuity rather than change as regards religious discrimination in Northern Ireland.

In 1989 the British government approved a new law on Fair Employment in Northern Ireland, and the Fair Employment Agency became the Fair Employment Commission. To some extent Britain was responding to pressure from the McBride Principles campaign, particularly in the US. Also, of course, there was a need to be seen to 'do something' about an issue which continued to fuel nationalist resentment. Yet the government's stated aim of achieving 'equality of opportunity' is not matched by the measures proposed which seem to centre on the professionalization of personnel practices, as though that was the sole, or even the main, issue. International experience with 'equal opportunities' programmes would suggest that a marked improvement in the position of Catholics in the labour market is unlikely to result. One indication of the government's uncertain outlook is its rejection of the advisory committee's recommendation that it should set a target of reducing Catholic's 2.5 times greater unemployment rate than Protestants to 1.5 times within five years. The government's White Paper concluded rather lamely that 'to set a target in terms of levels of unemployment would be to ignore the importance of the many variable and unpredictable factors which determine the overall unemployment level'.[27] So we find little decisive commitment to achieving an 'equality of outcome', without which 'equality of opportunity' does not mean all that much.

There have been some attempts to attribute inequality in employment to causes other than discrimination. Thus Paul Compton has argued that with rising unemployment, the growing Catholic population is more likely than the stable Protestant population to be jobless.[28] This, for Compton, is attributable to their numbers rather than any social injustice or barriers. However, this argument was rejected in a thorough 1987 Policy Studies Institute report, which found that:

> The increase in the rate of unemployment among Catholics between 1975 and 1983 is not consistent with any explanation substantively in terms of population growth, because it happened far too quickly to be explained in terms of the far more gradual growth of the Catholic population.[29]

In fact, this report found quite categorically that 'apart from discrimination' no other 'adequate explanation' exists for the very high levels of Catholic unemployment. Pointing to Catholic fertility rates usually leads to open or covert racism as with the Westminster MP who argued that: 'Many [Catholics] evidently believe in sponging off the state and do not want to work while others defraud the state by doing the double.'[30] Then, H. Shearman in the *Year Book of World Affairs* (1982) claimed that 'size of family . . . and other traceable habits of Roman Catholics, are mathematically sufficient to account for Roman Catholic disadvantage in employment without any need to suppose a significant factor of discrimination'.[31] Needless to say, no evidence was provided.

Unionist economist Tom Wilson has also tried to account for the years of discrimination under the Unionist state. Wilson refers to how 'some employers *believe* Protestant workers to be better at the job and more reliable than Catholics . . . [also] a preference for Protestants may reflect a belief that Protestant schools produce better trained pupils.'[32] He also argues that Catholics may be republicans, and, therefore, 'poor security risks'. If Protestants were better workers than Catholics, discrimination would not exist, because inequitable treatment would not be present. Wilson does admit that the Stormont government displayed sectarian bias internally but, he declares, 'It is hard to believe that there was any discrimination at all in its final phase.'[33] Against all the above equivocation and wishful thinking we can list the main mechanisms of discrimination as summarized by Rowthorn and Wayne:

1. Much industry is located in places which were difficult and dangerous for Catholics to reach;
2. Catholics who sought employment were less likely to be hired;
3. Once companies acquired the reputation of not hiring Catholics, Catholics stopped bothering to apply;
4. Some trade unions acted as hiring agents and constituted a hidden but effective barrier to Catholic recruitment;
5. There was frequently no public recruitment. Employers relied upon word-of-mouth hiring through existing staff and through other social contacts.[34]

Taken together these factors constitute a dense network of disadvantage and go a long way towards explaining the deeprootedness and perpetuation of religious imbalance at work.

5

The Agrarian Question

By Trutz Haase

Both political and economic development in Ireland continue to be strongly influenced by what happens in its agricultural sector. Historically, agrarian social relations crucially influenced the struggle of the Irish people for land and political sovereignty. Britain's vested interest in deriving profits from Irish land while simultaneously providing a guaranteed supply of agricultural produce to support its own drive towards industrialization was an equally important influence. Both factors together were pivotal in determining the particular form of Ireland's dependent development.

One-and-a-half centuries later, Ireland embarked on a new path of closer integration with international capitalism in general and away from an exclusive relationship with Britain. Despite the protective influence of the Common Agricultural Policy, subsequent upon joining the EC, agricultural production has continued to undergo dramatic changes which have not only fundamentally changed the role of agriculture within the Irish economy, but also deeply transformed social relations within rural Ireland. Today this development is set to accelerate even further, as the continuous support to finance high-price regimes and agricultural surplus production has become increasingly untenable for most of the member countries of the EC.

Agrarian transition

Contrary to popular myth, Irish history is not characterized by a united rural population in its struggle against inhuman conditions related to colonial rule. If one examines nineteenth-century rural unrest carefully, one finds that it did not consist of one continuous struggle but a number of different collective efforts by members of specific social groups whose interests were not identical and sometimes diametrically opposed. The majority of landlords in pre-Famine Ireland were not themselves landowners. Most were tenants with large holdings, subletting portions of their land to small occupiers. It was in fact this latter relationship between middlemen and their tenants which by reputation was far worse than that between landowners and their tenants.

Contrary to Malthusian views, the difficulty of tenants and landless labourers in maintaining a livelihood from the land was by no means the result of overpopulation. The concentration of the bulk of the Irish population in the poor western region and its subsequent 'congestion' had been the product of the enforced population movement and dispossession throughout the previous century. The re-allocation of land, following the revolution of 1688 against James II, had resulted in less than one-eleventh of the land area of Ireland being held by Catholics, and this small portion belonged to five or six families of English descent. As ownership of land was not possible for the Irish and being confronted with the rapid decline of the woollen industry as the result of the imposition of exorbitant taxes on exports, there was little else the majority of Irish people could do other than become landless labourers or emigrate. Where Catholics were able to rent land, tenancy was limited by law to a maximum of 31 years and the rent had to be at least two-thirds of the yield.

Catholic emancipation, introduced in 1829, only granted propertied Catholics the same rights as existed for propertied Protestants, but failed to bring alleviation for the farm labourers. Under these circumstances it was almost inevitable that the potato blight during the mid 1840s should lead to famine and mass emigration. But neither famine nor the serious agricultural depression between 1877 and 1889 was able to bring about a mass uprising of the Irish rural proletariat. Though the agricultural labourers experienced hardship, most large-scale collective action remained concentrated amongst the large tenant farmers. The Land League was dealing primarily with the insecurity of tenure, absentee landlordism, reclamation tenantry and freedom of contract. Its radical scheme for a major transformation of social relationships in Irish agriculture was frustrated by the mid 1880s. Their resistance to the consolidation of land and its subsequent use for pasture, which was of vital interest to the smaller farmers within the movement, did not lead to any major reorganization. In 1879 its leadership still believed that this could only be achieved when the British link was broken. Yet, as history showed, the objectives of the Land League were attainable, and were eventually attained, within the structure of the UK.

To understand the dissolution of landlordism and the emergence of peasant proprietorship in the late nineteenth century one has to look at the changes in social relationships that underlay the political events. Until the early 1820s Ireland had been the main supplier of grain for the English market. As cheaper Canadian grain became available around this time, the resulting shift in demand forced Irish farmers to gradually change from tillage to pasture. This in turn accelerated the steady decline in the demand for agricultural labour. The widespread hostility among the landless labourers towards grazing, and farmers who specialized in grazing, indicates that they were well aware of the danger that pasture farming represented to their interests.

Whilst the substitution of tillage by pasture partly created the pre-conditions for the Famine to occur, the Famine itself reinforced that shift. In the wake of the Great Famine, Ireland's population had declined by more than a third between 1841 and 1881 and the average size of holdings had almost doubled. This resulted in a tremendous growth of pasture farming. Even small landholders in the west now became involved in livestock farming, though mainly in breeding and rearing, whilst the large landholders in the east engaged in the more profitable activity of fattening and exporting. The effects on the class structure were a substantial decline in the practice of sub-letting land and a marked decline in the number of agricultural labourers.

However, Catholics still remained largely excluded from owning the land they worked. The Landlord and Tenant Law Amendment Act, 1860 (Deasy's Act) reinforced the landlords' powers to recover land without notice or compensation for improvement. Equally the effects of the disestablishment of the Church of Ireland were not as far reaching as often believed. Less than 7,000 out of the national total of 593,000 tenants gained ownership of their holdings at this stage. By 1870, though it was meanwhile possible for Catholics to own land, the whole of Ireland outside its towns still belonged to less than 20,000 landlords, 6,000 of whom owned more than half of the land. The first of Gladstone's Landlord and Tenant Acts in 1870 had given the tenants compensation for their improvements and for some evictions. But the Act did not foresee compensation in cases of eviction for arrears of rent, still leaving three-quarters of the tenants effectively at the will of their landlords.

Only after the Land War, which lasted from 1871 to 1882, had the balance of class forces shifted qualitatively. In 1881 the Land Law Act generalized what had been known as the 'Ulster custom' until then, establishing a form of dual ownership between landlord and tenant; the latter having the right to enhanced value in sale of improved lands. This act marked not only the first real step towards the abolition of landlordism but, in contrast to England, also the simultaneous emergence of peasant proprietorship. Furthermore, it effectively shelved demands for the collectivization of land as expressed in the demands for nationalization by parts of the Land League which would have been in the interest of the landless labourers. Finally, the Act's forbidding of land sub-divisions drew a final line between small tenants and landless labourers.

The Land League effectively fell apart over the Act. The landless labourers, under the leadership of Davitt, briefly joined the labour movement, reiterating the demand for land nationalization but surrendered the principal demand later in favour of piecemeal reforms. Balfour's Land Act of 1891 marks the conscious attempt to create the conditions for a conservative peasantry to kill the call for Home Rule. In 1899 a special Irish Department of Agriculture and Technical Instruction was set up to relieve congestion and to improve production in agriculture. One of its central policy proposals was the transformation of the tenantry into a class of peasant proprietors, which subsequently was carried through under Wyndham's Land Act of 1903. Within six years 270,000 out of the remaining odd 500,000 tenants bought their holdings.

Southern Ireland gained its political independence in 1922, despite the fact that the objectives of the Land League had been eventually attained within the structure of the United Kingdom. The social transformation, initiated as the last attempt to maintain British sovereignty in Ireland, had been a radical one. In 1870 only 3 per cent of those who worked the land owned it, whereas in 1921 the figure had reached 64 per cent. By 1923 the agrarian 'revolution' was complete and the new farming class was to be the backbone of the newly established Free State.

Agriculture after partition

Ireland's economic performance since the 1920s in many ways resembles the development of other neo-colonial countries. Weakened by its inherited pattern of agricultural production, the structural deformities of land tenure and the effects of colonization resulting in the subsequent partition of Ireland, continuous underdevelopment seems to have been the inevitable outcome.

The profitability of extensive farming depended on access to British markets, making the big farmers of the east ardent free traders. The development strategy adopted by the first Irish government reflects this relationship by placing its emphasis on maintaining the pre-existing economic, financial and trading links with the United Kingdom. This has two consequences: firstly, predominance of extensive farming, itself a result of the peripheralization experienced under colonial domination, continued uninterrupted into the new era; and secondly, the access to British markets was only part of the free trade environment. Two other aspects were that no tariff protection was available for Irish infant industry and that capital itself remained highly mobile. Agricultural surpluses, which were previously expatriated through excessive rents, were now deposited in the banks, which in turn invested these in safe British government securities rather than reinvesting into the Irish economy. Irish industry was exposed to the full blast of competition from developed British industry and at the same time was starved of capital.

The dominance of agricultural interests reflected the fact that, in contrast to other countries in which the bourgeoisie had emerged with the industrial sector, the Irish Catholic bourgeoisie had emerged out of agriculture and trade. Already, before the turn of the century, the Irish Local Government Act of 1898 had marked the decisive shift in power and influence away from the landlord ascendancy class and towards the larger farmers, shopkeepers and publicans. The strength of this newly arising class also became apparent when in early 1918 provincial Sinn Fein, based largely on labourers and small farmers, openly fought to break up the great grazing farms. For the land-hungry small men of the west this essentially meant seizure of estates and redistribution of the pasture of the large ranchers to smallholders and landless men. More immediately it meant access to conacre land for survival. However, they were not supported by the Republican leadership which, at critical moments like this, found it more important to reassure the alliance with the men of property. The dominant view among the Sinn Fein leadership was that the political question – that is, the constitutional status of the Irish state – should be the primary issue in the struggle for independence, avoiding socially divisive questions such as land reform.

None the less the 'men of substance' had cause for anxiety and as early as 1917 the more substantial farmers organized themselves in the Irish Farmers' Union (IFU). Their aim was to resist the wage demands of agricultural labourers which, with ever greater urgency and power, had been voiced by the Irish Transport and General Workers Union (ITGWU) and the Trade Councils. By spring 1919 the IFU and the ITGWU were already locked in vigorous conflict over agricultural wages and conditions in Meath and Kildare. Numerous wage agreements were consequently signed between the two organizations, most of them in the richer counties of Leinster with their large work forces. Furthermore, the IFU was strictly opposed to the extension of state controls, for example tillage controls, which it saw as the first step 'towards nationalization of the land'. In contrast, this did not prevent the IFU from calling on the state when it suited them, as in the question of rates and the non-payment of land annuities.

After partition, the division of opinion over the direction which agricultural policy should take was reflected in the Majority and Minority Reports of the 1923 Commission on Agriculture. While the Majority proposed that state funds should be channelled towards the improvement of efficiency in the production and marketing of agricultural produce, the Minority favoured a more interventionist policy to increase tillage and to encourage the expansion of resource-based industries. Both approaches eventually failed. As agricultural employment inevitably fell as the result of improved productivity, the failure to create alternative employment proved disastrous. Net emigration continued to be a consistent feature of Irish society, hitting particularly the rural areas. While the total population of the state was exactly the same in 1971 as in 1926, at 2.98 million, this figure conceals a net growth of 72 per cent in urban areas and a fall of 31 per cent in rural areas, with much heavier declines in particular counties.

As regards agricultural policy the politics of the Fianna Fail government, which came to power in 1932 with considerable support from small farmer interests, proved to be more efficient. The support of certain crops, particularly wheat and sugar-beet, did not bring about an increase in the overall acreage under tillage. The increase in supported crops was offset by a corresponding decline in other crops. Another side effect of the government policy was that, due to the sharp fall in agricultural prices in the wake of the Economic War, the farming sector responded with a decline in the proportion of output sold off-farm, thereby further manifesting subsistence-type farming.

The Common Market

At least since the early 1950s it had become apparent that for many reasons agriculture was unable to play the dominant role for the Irish economy which it had in the past. As is the case in all developing countries, agricultural employment in Ireland is characterized by a steady long-run decline. This is because agriculture, in general, is subject to rather low and even declining income elasticities of demand. As personal income grows, people spend a decreasing proportion of their income on food. Whilst, at least in theory, the manufacturing sector can expand almost arbitrarily, the agricultural sector lacks the dynamism to generate sufficient new employment for a rapidly growing population. Particularly since the Second World War, growth rates in agricultural labour productivity, due to improved produce development and increasing mechanization, have been in excess of those in industry and services. This has resulted in the continuous decline of agriculture's share in GDP and a corresponding decline in the agricultural labour force.

However, whilst this process is characteristic for all developing countries, this process occurs neither as a constant change over time, nor does it affect all countries or regions in exactly the same way; rather it develops as a highly uneven process. A brief look at the decline in Irish agricultural employment may exemplify this: between 1926 and 1946 agricultural employment in the South fell by 85,000 or by about 3.5 per cent every five years. In the postwar period of 1946 to 1961 this rate jumped to over 14 per cent every five years, exactly four times that of the prewar period.

As we have seen in earlier chapters, the search for an alternative growth policy, which would not question the capitalist basis of the economic system, resulted in the adoption of a strategy of more comprehensive integration with international capitalism. The qualitative changes in the shift from international trade to international production, following the Second World War, provided the necessary background for this new strategy, based largely on attracting foreign-owned companies oriented towards the export market. The drive towards greater integration finally culminated in the accession of Ireland and – in the case of the North – the UK to the European Community in 1973. Hopes were flying high as the EC's practical intervention had largely concentrated around its Common Agricultural

Policy (CAP) and it was widely believed that agriculture in Ireland would greatly benefit under the prevailing support regimes.

Almost two decades later it is striking that the issues of low and volatile incomes in the agricultural sectors North and South have essentially remained unchanged. Windfall profits during the initial years, consequent upon adapting to the high price regimes under the CAP, were inevitably short lived. Dairying and beef, Ireland's two major product markets, were already in surplus supply or approaching self-sufficiency at the European level at the time of entry. Profit margins in the intensive livestock sector, which was of particular importance to Northern agriculture, slumped as high prices for agricultural produce equally affected input costs. In total, despite a period of strong growth in agricultural incomes during the early years, farming incomes have remained far below industrial wages and disparities in agricultural incomes between farms and regions have remained profound and continue to widen.

In the South, today, 25 per cent of farms account for 75 per cent of agricultural production. In the North the contrast is of almost the same proportion, with 30 per cent of farms accounting for 70 per cent of production. The CAP has done little to alleviate this divide. By far the largest proportion of spending under the CAP has been used to sustain high price regimes as the principle means to support agricultural incomes. Thus the farmer who already has greater resources attracts more funding. Equally, farm modernization schemes, introduced to raise farm incomes to a comparable level with non-agricultural wages, often directly discriminated against farmers below a certain threshold and against part-time farmers.

The effect has been a process of increasing specialization and unprecedented concentration of production in every product group of agricultural production. The figures below demonstrate this process in the case of the North's dairy industry. Between 1971 and 1987 the number of dairy cows grew from under 220,000 to nearly 290,000. However, over the same period the number of farms with dairy cows dropped from just over 14,000 to about 7,000 in 1987. A similar concentration process has taken place in the intensive livestock sector. By the late 1980s, 4 per cent of pig-producing farms contained almost half of the North's pig population in herds of over 1,000 and half of these herds were over 2,000 in size. In the poultry industry nearly 60 per cent of the egg-laying flock of almost 2 million hens were concentrated in just over 1 per cent of egg-producing farms.

Not surprisingly, the pressure on the marginal farmer has remained unchanged, if not become worse. Between 1973 and 1987 agricultural employment in the South dropped by almost 100,000 with the share of agriculture in total employment falling from 24 to 15 per cent. Effectively every third person involved in farming at the time of joining EC had given up his/her occupation within less than fifteen years. In the North the decline was not quite as severe with some 20 per cent reduction in the agricultural labour force, but this still meant that over 10,000 people left their traditional occupation.

The close integration into the capitalist world economy had unleashed profound changes in the social relations within Irish agriculture. Worldwide, agriculture had, since the Second World War, increasingly become differentiated into distinct input, food-raising and food-processing and marketing sectors. With the opening-up of the Irish economy, capital penetration into agriculture was now allowed to occur suddenly and as a highly uneven process. Within less than 20 years the input, processing and marketing sectors have become dominated by large capitalist corporations. Simultaneously, the food-raising sector has become minimized in its relative importance to the agricultural sector as a whole, hence reducing the bargaining power of farmers in general and particularly that of smaller farmers. This process has been actively supported by individual governments and the EC as a whole through the subsidizing of capital investment in agriculture and through policies on farm modernization and income support. The public emphasis given to the special role of the family farm, in contrast, cannot be seen other than largely a rhetorical exercise, aimed at containing potential social unrest in response to the uprooting of traditional farming structures.

Despite their formal independence, the vast majority of farmers are today completely subsumed into the capitalist system. The owners of the smaller and medium-sized farms experience increasing marginalization within a rapidly changing environment. Unable to expand their food production and in the absence of alternative employment opportunities most of them are compelled to either hold on to their unviable holdings or to join the unemployment queues.

Rural development

Today it is more apparent than ever that the problems of low farming incomes and high unemployment in rural areas, whilst partly originating from within the agricultural sector, are essentially regional problems and that their solution will have to encompass all sectors of the rural community. As far back as 1968 the Commission of the European Community for the first time put forward a coherent strategy on structural issues such as the levels of investment and the size of farms. The most radical element of the Mansholt Plan was the argument that about 5 million farmers in the six original member states would need to leave the industry during the 1970s if it were to become efficient enough to generate adequate income without reliance on artificially raised prices. Politically the plan proved impossible to be carried through as it met radical opposition from all sides. The CAP, as it subsequently developed, effectively protected farmers to some extent against the rigour of the market forces. This, however introduced a contradiction within the aims of the CAP: on the one hand the CAP provides production subsidies and hence allows more farmers to stay on the land than would otherwise be the case; on the other hand, the principal aim of creating, in the long run, efficient farm businesses with a resource mix which will allow them to compete on the world market remained. Not surprisingly, the CAP had been riddled with this contradiction for the beginning. Price policies were dominant and yet did not provide genuine support for small farmers. At the same time the almost exclusive reliance on output-related subsidies left few financial resources for improving farming structures directly.

Today, it is widely accepted that the CAP must be reformed; there is less agreement on how this should be done . In 1985 the Commission of the EC admitted in its Green Paper on the perspectives for the CAP that support prices could not perform the dual role of stabilizing markets and supporting agricultural incomes. They recommended a more market-oriented price policy and the development of new forms of income support for the agricultural sector. However, despite the disastrous effect on marginal producers, neither the introduction of quotas nor greater selectivity in the application of the intervention brought down the overall CAP spending. This may change now, under the pressure of the latest round of talks on the General Agreement on Tariffs and Trade (GATT). The EC's major trading partners (in particular the US) have demanded that the EC radically reduce their agricultural support. At the time of writing it has not yet become clear what the ultimate outcome of the negotiations will be, but it is likely to centre around substantial reductions in agricultural supports between 1993–9; including a reduction of 36 per cent in all non-tariff import barriers and export subsidies; and a reduction of 20 per cent in all domestic supports.

The major question posed by the GATT negotiations relates to the extent to which compensations will be made available to farmers in return for the price reductions. Unless these are allowed it is doubtful if the proposals would be acceptable to the Agricultural Ministers as farmers' incomes would be depressed to unacceptably low levels. It therefore looks as if farmers' incomes may be protected for the interim time of the implementation of the GATT proposals. After that, however, structurally less competitive farms will inevitable be hit by the downward pressure on agricultural commodity prices. Furthermore, as income subsidies will not be transferable to the next generation, at least in the longer run many of the small to medium sized farms are likely to cease to exist.

Not surprisingly, as agriculture faces an uncertain future, there has emerged an increasing emphasis on rural development to stem the tide of rural outmigration. This change in emphasis is also reflected in the growing importance given to the structural funds within the Community Support Framework, Such a shift could potentially be beneficial for rural areas. Rather than narrowly focusing on agricultural support, which even in the most rural areas benefits only a minority of the population, it would create the possibility for coordination of agricultural measures with broader measures of regional and social policy. In particular it would allow for the targeting of support towards the most disadvantaged of the rural population, as well as the inclusion of environmental concerns.

In the interim, however, it leaves rural areas in a dilemma. The decline in support for agriculture has been occurring for over a decade and seems likely to even accelerate. New measures which are being developed have not yet taken effect. The structural component of the agricultural funds still accounts for only 7 per cent of its total. Even after the doubling of the combined Structural Funds by 1993, they will amount to only one-third of 1 per cent of the Community's GDP, hardly enough to make a serious impression.

6

Europe and 1992

With the prospect of a Single European Market looming ever larger on the horizon it becomes imperative to carry out a cool, dispassionate analysis of its likely impact on the Irish economies, North and South. However, rather than launch immediately into a consideration of the Single European Market and its implications, we should commence with a retrospective balance-sheet of the consequences of accession to the European Economic Community (EC) in 1973 by the two parts of Ireland.

The move towards unification of the Western European economies began in the aftermath of the Second World War. The waste and destruction caused by two world wars drove some of the major postwar leaders to seek an economic and political integration of their respective nation-states. This pressure led to the setting up of the Council of Europe in 1949 to promote federalism, but since it lacked real power this organization did not prosper. However, by 1951 the European Coal and Steel Community had been formed to rationalize production of these goods in France, West Germany, Italy and the Benelux countries (Belgium, Netherlands and Luxembourg). Britain stayed out of this organization on the basis that the Empire (even then on its last legs) and the 'special relationship' with the United States made any participation in European integration unnecessary. The Republic of Ireland, still firmly linked to the British economy, followed suit.

The original six countries which formed the European Coal and Steel Community eventually became the European Economic Community (EC) in 1958. In 1961, Britain and the Republic applied simultaneously to join the EC, the latter fearing that its agricultural exports to Britain would suffer if it did not go along. However, French President De Gaulle vetoed Britain's application. After another unsuccessful application in 1967 Britain and Ireland finally joined the EC in 1973, with popular support being considerably greater in Ireland. The Republic was set to gain from the EC's Common Agricultural Policy (CAP) whereas Britain was to become a net contributor to the EC budget. Northern Ireland in this respect had more in common with the Republic than with Britain. The attractions of membership for the two Irish economies were considerable. The CAP would guarantee high prices and secure access for Irish agricultural exports to the EC markets. Even the expectation that free trade would lead to job losses in the home market seemed to be compensated for by the prospect of tariff-free access to EC markets by the new breed of export-oriented firms. Membership of the EC was thought to be beneficial in attracting foreign investors who would see Ireland as an 'export platform' to launch their products into Europe. Furthermore, Ireland's status as the least developed nation in Europe would qualify it for the major share of regional grants. Even the potential loss of sovereignty implicit in joining a supra-national body such as the EC would be compensated by participation in decision making at a European level.

Critics of the EC pointed out the economic and political dangers for countries such as Ireland. As Anthony Coughlan notes, 'They feared that the EEC's farm structure programme would be oriented against small-scale producers. [And] that the CAP would be eroded in time by the pressure of consumer interests.'[1] Critics also pointed to the difficulty of the weak Irish state countering the tendency towards concentration of economic (and political) power in the central more advanced countries of Europe. In this context it seemed unlikely that Irish firms would be able to compete on an equal footing and generate the jobs required by a rapidly rising population. More generally, radical critics of the EC pointed to its origins as an association of ex-colonial powers, and its implications for the Republic's policy of non-alignment and military neutrality. In the North, as Paul Hainsworth notes, 'Europe represented a potential and alien threat to Northern Ireland's existence'[2] as far as Unionists were concerned. Nationalists, immersed in a bitter conflict for survival, viewed the EC as merely a diversion. Overall, we can note a fear that accession to the EC would lead to a diminution of sovereignty and a certain scepticism as to the ability of any short-term benefits to counter the long-term detrimental economic effects of centralization on an international scale.

Before assessing the results of EC membership for Ireland since 1973 it is necessary to provide some basic information on the EC, if only to make sense of later references. We noted above the process leading up to formation of the EC in 1958. The primary objective was the economic integration of the member states, that is the combination of their economies to form a larger, more powerful, European economy. The purpose of this exercise was to improve the economic welfare of its members. A related objective was to promote political integration between the member states. One of the major prerequisites of economic integration, a zone of monetary stability within Europe, was only achieved in 1979 with the formation of the European Monetary System (EMS). Significantly, Britain with its traditional links to the dollar system and its significant financial sector (the City) remained outside the EMS until late in 1990, and thus hampered the moves towards a more stable exchange-rate regime within the Community. Britain's recent withdrawl from the EMS and the financial upheavals in the Republic shows that this problem is ongoing. Nor to date has the EC achieved the status of being a common market, with restrictions on trade still playing a major role. This failure, or at least incomplete achievement, of the EC's original agenda lies behind the present initiative for achieving a single European market.

The CAP has been the EC policy with the most direct influence on Ireland. The aims of the CAP as set out in the Treaty of Rome (which established the EC) include: to increase agricultural productivity, to stabilize markets and to ensure reasonable consumer prices. To meet these objectives the CAP operates a number of mechanisms for agricultural price support in order to maintain farm incomes, although the use of quotas to control surplus production has become increasingly important since the late 1980s. Commonly, the CAP has been viewed as a means by which France has made the other European countries carry the burden of its antiquated agrarian structure. A more accurate interpretation would emphasize the general interest of the EC in minimizing its dependence on that strategic commodity, food. Moreover, even what are seen as advanced economies (such as what was West Germany) have a significant number of people who farm part-time but also have 'full-time' jobs in industry. One political effect of this characteristic is the maintenance of a sizeable political constituency on the land which can act as a bulwark against any threat from the left. Nevertheless the CAP has generally been recognized to be in crisis in recent years. The striking absurdity of 'food mountains' and 'wine lakes' is but one symptom of a growing crisis of overproduction, while at the same time farmers are increasingly being driven from the land due to mechanization and concentration of holdings.

Another major area of EC policy which impacts on Ireland is the various regional funds. The Treaty of Rome had stated that the EC members 'are anxious to strengthen the unity of their economies and to ensure their harmonious development by reducing the differences between the various regions and by mitigating the backwardness of the less favoured regions'. To this end the European Investment Bank (EIB) was set up when the EC was formed, although it was not until 1975 that the more specific European Regional Development Fund (ERDF) was established to assist regional development. It was a limited initiative, accounting for less than 5 per cent of the Community budget, and faced an insurmountable contradiction. On the one hand, uneven development within the EC had created major disparities between the prosperous and underdeveloped areas. This was considered by some to be socially unjust and politically unacceptable. On the other hand, regional policies represented a threat to the principle of free competition and trade on which the EC was based. The contradiction was accentuated by what is known as the 'second enlargement' of the EC in 1986 when Spain and Portugal joined (Greece having joined in 1981), thus enlarging the peripheral or relatively underdeveloped areas of the EC.

Effects of EC membership

We noted above that the perceived benefits of the CAP were a major motivation for Ireland's accession to the EC. Indeed, initially the most striking economic effect of EC membership in the South was the rise in farm incomes, with agricultural prices trebling between 1973 and 1980. With milk prices rising faster than cattle prices – against the traditional trend – small- and medium-sized dairying farms were even able to hold their own against the more land-intensive cattle-rearing sector. However, contrary to expectations, EC membership did not eliminate the production cycles typical of the sector. Furthermore, when the EC began to introduce milk quotas this hit Irish farming disproportionately due to the greater reliance on dairying in Ireland, compared to other European regions.

An official survey of Irish agriculture notes how the EC:

did, indeed, bring prosperity to its farming and rural areas. Anyone who had seen the countryside in, say the nineteen fifties and had not seen it again until, say, 1978, would have been struck by the transformation. Social conditions, though still modest by comparison with some of its better-off neighbours on the continent had changed radically for the better.[3]

Short- and long-term farm investment was taking place. The increased income of farmers also brought contractors and shopkeepers in the country town a veritable boom. Yet the other side of the coin, as noted by Coughlan, is that: 'Irish land prices rose to be the highest in Europe (double British levels) which made it more difficult for young, active people, those most likely to use land effectively, to enter farming.'4 So, at the moment when the farming sector was benefiting most from the EC accession, the doors were being closed to younger farmers.

Even bearing in mind such contradictory effects, the relative prosperity of agriculture in the first years of EC membership was eventually to come to an end. From 1978 to 1984 agriculture in the South of Ireland operated in an extremely unfavourable economic climate, with high inflation and interest rates and a deepening recession and rate of unemployment. One official report notes how by 1980: 'The average farm family income dropped in real terms by over one-third, to a level below that which had prevailed in 1972 before Ireland joined the community.'5 In the 1980s there were periods of relative recovery (1982–4) followed by renewed depression (1985–6), but the simple picture of uniformly increasing prosperity under the EC was essentially over.

Agriculture in Northern Ireland follows a similar pattern to that of the South, particularly compared to Britain which is, of course, a net food importer. As in the South, the initial windfalls from the EC led farmers into buying more land and investing. However, the income of many farmers has remained meagre partly as a result of the terms of trade within the EC moving against agricultural produce. Subsequent rises in input costs and restrictions on output (mainly through the introduction of milk quotas in 1984) led inevitably to increased farm insolvencies. Of course, while some farmers lost out others benefited. One example was noted in Chapter 5 where we saw that while the number of cows in the six counties increased steadily between the 1960s and 1970s, the number of herds is now one-third of what it was in 1964. That is to say, two-thirds of the dairy herds in the North have simply disappeared. Similar developments have taken place in other sectors. Today, an increasing proportion of pig production is carried out as a single 'birth to bacon' enterprise. In 1973, pigs were held on over 16,000 farms – today that figure has declined to 3,600 farms. Similarly nearly 80 per cent of poultry are today concentrated in flocks greater than 10,000 birds. From this point of view, possibly only one-third of farmers in Ireland have actually benefited from accession to the EC.

Developments in Irish agriculture could have been foreseen in 1973, insofar as the EC was already self-sufficient in all of Ireland's major agricultural products at that stage. But the CAP was always about more than its stated aim of providing a fair living standard to the whole agricultural community. The CAP was intended to assist the orderly re-structuring of agriculture in the EC. Market pressures were leading to a growing concentration of holdings and modernization of procedures in any event. The price-guarantee mechanisms of the CAP actually accelerated this process while the structural policies (which were intended to promote alternative means of support for the rural population) remained comparatively underfunded and ineffective. So, in the South agricultural employment fell by 35 per cent between 1973 and 1985 and in the North by 17 per cent over the same period. Since they were related to volume of output, the price-support mechanisms of CAP by their very nature favoured the large farmer. As 25 per cent of farms account for 75 per cent of production, the better-off farmers clearly have done best. Those driven off the land have been less fortunate. In recent years pressure for reform of the CAP has risen to extreme levels both from within the Community (where CAP expenditure prevents a rational development of the Community budget) and from outside (for example, in the GATT negotiations where legitimate Third World criticisms of the CAP have combined with more opportunistic criticism from countries such as the US). Despite these pressures for change those with vested interests in the status-quo are fighting a vigorous campaign against even the modest reforms proposed by the EC's own Commissioner for Agriculture.

Moving on to look at the manufacturing sector we must consider whether Ireland's entry into the EC led to the hoped for influx of foreign investment. Foreign firms now account for over 40 per cent of all jobs in the manufacturing sector, 50 per cent of manufacturing output and 75 per cent of industrial exports in the Republic. In some sectors the extent of foreign ownership is above the average – for example, 75 per cent of employment in chemicals and 70 per cent of employment in the drink and tobacco industry is foreign owned. The US holds the largest share of foreign investment in the Republic – owning 357 of the 986 foreign-owned manufacturing firms in 1990. As the Economist Intelligence Unit notes: 'This reflects a rapid expansion of new US investment during the latter half of the 1970s in the electronics and other high technology sectors, such as chemicals and pharmaceuticals, using Ireland as an export base within the European Community.'[6] Britain is the second most important investment source, accounting for approximately one-quarter of manufacturing firms. However, reflecting the pattern of previous relations between Britain and Ireland, this investment is concentrated in the production of consumer goods (such as food, clothing and household products). These firms had been established in Ireland before the Republic moved away from tariff barriers to protect local industry and adopted what is known as an outward-oriented economic policy. Germany, the now dominant European economy, is third in importance in Ireland, accounting for 15 per cent of the total number of foreign-owned manufacturing firms. Table 6.1 provides some more detail on foreign investment in the Republic.

Table 6.1: Nationality of Foreign-owned Manufacturing Companies in the Republic, 1990

Nationality	Companies		Employment	
	No.	*%*	*No.*	*%*
US	357	36.2	43,800	48.3
Canada	25	12.5	2,800	3.1
UK	225	22.8	16,900	18.6
West Germany	151	15.3	11,500	12.7
Netherlands	50	5.1	2,400	2.6
Sweden	28	2.8	2,100	2.3
Japan	14	1.4	1,900	2.1
Others	136	13.8	9,300	10.3
Total	986	100.0	90,700	100.0

Source: Department of Industry and Commerce, 1990.

Interestingly Japan does not emerge as such as important investor as commonly imagined. The US, when combined with largely Canadian investment, accounts for just over half of all employment in this sector. Apart from West Germany, other European countries – in order of importance: the Netherlands, Sweden, France, Switzerland and Denmark – are now beginning to have a significant impact. We should ask the question whether the inflow of foreign capital to the South in the 1970s was actually due to accession to the EC. Certainly, had the Republic remained outside the EC some form of free-trade arrangements – as Switzerland and the Scandinavian countries have – would have been implemented. Foreign investors find the South of Ireland a profitable location, due to the generous package of investment grants and tax relief offered and the relatively stable political situation. As the Economist Intelligence Unit notes: 'The attitude towards foreign investment has remained positive, and has been largely above political debate'.[7] What changed with Ireland's accession to the EC in 1973 was a turn in investment patterns from labour-intensive projects to more technologically advanced projects for export to the UK and the rest of Europe.

Table 6.2: Foreign Firms in Northern Ireland, 1958–90

		Country of Origin			
Year	*US*	*Canada*	*West Germany*	*Other European*	*South Africa*
1958	7	–	–	6	–
1968	27	1	5	9	1
1975	26	2	11	11	1
1990	30	3	9	16	–

Source: Department of Economic Development and Industrial Development Board for Northern Ireland, various years.

In Northern Ireland the question of foreign investment follows similar patterns, although it is more affected by its status as a depressed region of the UK. Table 6.2 gives some idea of the evolution of foreign investment in Northern Ireland (British investment being, of course, difficult to distinguish from local). The table shows that before 1968 foreign investment increased markedly but that since then expansion has been modest, although European firms have increased significantly. As with the South, a generous package of grants and regional incentives favoured this increase in foreign investments, but it is difficult to assess the precise influence of accession to the EC in 1973. Foreign investment was concentrated in the mechanical and electrical industries, engineering and the textiles industrial sectors. Already by the 1970s foreign firms were clearly the core dynamic sector of the North's economy.

By the mid 1970s the oil crisis, inflation and the continuing troubles all combined to bring the apparently prosperous outlook for foreign firms to an end. Since then, the number of multinational companies operating in Northern Ireland has decreased with monotonous regularity. Whereas even as late as 1981, foreign-owned enterprises had accounted for 30 per cent of gross value added to the North's economy, this proportion had decreased to 19 per cent in 1983 and had been falling since. Between 1981 and 1985, 5 US firms were established in the North, but 12 firms closed down. Significantly 9 Irish firms opened in the North during this same period, largely by acquisition of existing plants. Overall, multinational investment in Northern Ireland has created very few 'backward linkages' into the local economy, and they have tended to be low-technology concerns requiring a semi-skilled workforce. Certainly, there are no grounds for assuming that increased foreign investment will be a panacea for the North's economic ills.

Given the disparate levels of social and economic development within the EC, the issue of how uneven development is dealt with is crucial. The Republic has been classified as 'underdeveloped' in terms of EC regional aids and Northern Ireland recognized as a depressed region within the UK. It could be expected, therefore, that 15 years of EC membership could have gone some way towards alleviating regional disparities between Ireland and the rest of the Community.

The European Commission itself has carried out periodic reviews of the EC regions to assess whether convergence of income levels across them has, in fact, been taking place. The Commission's *Fourth Periodic Report* of 1991 found that the Republic had the highest unemployment rate in the EC, being just higher than that of Spain (Commission of the European Communities, 1991). The fact that we should treat these comparisons with caution is, however, underlined by the changing position of the UK in relation to unemployment. In the four years between the publication of the *Fourth Periodic Report* and its predecessor, the unemployment statistics for the UK appeared to improve dramatically. In fact much of the apparent improvement during this period was due to a series of changes in the techniques used to measure unemployment. A broader measure of the relative prosperity of regions in the EC is Gross Domestic Product (GDP) per head of population figures for 1986–8. These figures show that the Republic ranked 25th poorest region, with 64.5 per cent of the average income in the Community, while Northern Ireland was in 45th place, with a

GDP of 80.6 per cent of the Community average. We should note, however, that GDP only measures the product accruing to nationals of an economy. In the Republic, in particular, the amount of GDP lost abroad through repatriation of profits by foreign investors is considerable. For example, the proportion deducted from the GDP in the Republic in this way rose from 3 per cent in 1980 to 11 per cent in 1986.

Ranking regions according to unemployment rates and income per head of population does not really provide a complete picture of social and economic development. Consequently, the EC devised a composite measure of the intensity of regional problems. This synthetic index, as it is known, includes an assessment of the regions' productivity, underemployment as well as unemployment, and a dynamic element, considering prospective labour force changes to 1990. According to this evaluation, the Republic emerged as the 6th weakest region and Northern Ireland as the 33rd weakest of a total of 160. Taking a broad historical view of the regions in the EC we find a certain tendency towards convergence prior to 1974 but from then onwards the dominant trend has been towards divergence between the richest and poorest regions. As the European Commission itself reports: 'Taken together, the above analyses show that, in terms of the distribution of economic activity within the Community, the peripheral regions display a series of attributes that place them in a distinctly less favourable position than other regions.'[8]

Since joining the EC in 1973 both parts of Ireland have received substantial clash inflows from the various EC funds. The sources and amounts can be seen in Table 6.3. The South has also made considerable use of the Community loan instruments (mainly the European Investment Bank), amounting to I£281m in 1982 for example, whereas Northern Ireland has made minimal use of the bank. Though obviously significant, these EC grants need to be placed in context. The Republic did, indeed, go through a marked process of 'catching up' with the EC during the first five years of membership. However, by the 1980s, this process had 'come to a virtual halt' according to the EC itself. The funds received from the EC have been disappointing, with the exception of the CAP. According to Coughlan: 'The sums received from the two funds [Regional and Social] have amounted to about 2 per cent of current government spending in the years since joining. Spread over many small projects, they can only be regarded as gestures towards a regional policy.'[9] With the Republic classed as a depressed region in its entirety, the question of regional development within the 26 counties

**Table 6.3: Receipts and Payments from the EC Budget,
1982–6 (£m Stg)**

Year	ERDF		ESF		EAGGF	
	North	South	North	South	North	South
1982	17.6	53.54	32.65	59.29	6.88	48.28
1983	14.64	47.72	37.3	76.01	14.08	52.23
1984	15.98	52.89	38.0	68.28	15.02	39.93
1985	18.0	62.32	28.25	115.87	15.18	45.77
1986	22.0	70.16	46.23	115.12	10.34	41.86

Note: ESF – European Social Fund; EAGGF – European Agricultural Guidance and
Guarantee Fund.

Source: NESC 1989, Hansard 1990.

has not been addressed. One of the main side effects of the manner in
which the ERDF has been administered in the South has been the
reinforcement of the role of central government in regional planning.
Thus, regional and local authorities have been particularly ineffective
in influencing the deployment of the Regional Fund across the country.
This is, in fact, against the Commission's objective of having regional
and local involvement at national level planning of regional development. The prospects for an effective EC regional policy do not seem
particularly bright judging by developments in the South to date. Recent
discussions between the member of states of the EC on developing
closer economic, monetary and political union have provoked Ireland,
Spain, Portugal and Greece to demand greater resources for regional
development. Whether an effective change along these lines actually
comes about remains to be seen.

In Northern Ireland, a major issue has been the refusal of the British
government to implement the 'additionality' principle, whereby EC
funds were supposed to be extra to regional development funds. By and
large, Britain has appeared to use EC regional assistance to compensate
for public expenditure which would have occurred in any event in the
North. Though Northern Ireland has done well out of the Regional Fund
per capita compared to, say, Scotland and Wales, the overall impact has

not been dramatic. A report by Paul Hainsworth on this subject concluded that: 'The overall impression of the EC's funding is that with the exception of farming guarantees, it is very marginal to the Northern Ireland economy.'[10] Compared to the financial links with Britain, the EC funds are, indeed, of little import. In this context, it is hardly surprising that the report cited above concluded that: 'The political mileage to be gained from the EC's grants appears infinitely greater than the actual effects of the various grants.'[11] The way in which particular projects – such as the Foyle Bridge – are claimed by the region's MEP, testify to the validity of this conclusion to date. None the less, both the political and economic effects of EC regional policy are of increasing importance and the eventual impact of this policy on relations between the member states and their constituent regions, though still unclear, could well result in fundamental change.

With Britain and the Republic of Ireland both part of the EC, it seemed logical to assume that the border between the two parts of Ireland might fade in significance. Unionists in Northern Ireland perceived the end of the local parliament at Stormont in 1972 and the subsequent entry into the EC as linked disasters. Whereas the Social Democratic and Labour Party (SDLP) supported the idea of a united Ireland within an EC context, the Unionists campaigned vigorously for a negative vote in the 1975 Referendum on the EC. For example, the leader of the local 'Get Britain Out' campaign declared that:

> Just as we are prepared to live in peace with mutual respect and toleration for out fellow countrymen on one island, but never in one Ireland, we are willing to live together on one continent but not in any one Community.[12]

Thus for Unionists, Europe represented a potential and alien threat to the very existence of the Northern Ireland state. The reality of cross-border cooperation between the two Irish states, in the context of the EC, has been less dramatic.

A survey of cross-border cooperation carried out by the New Ireland Forum in 1983 notes that:

> Apart from seeking EC financial support for cross-border studies, the British and Irish Governments have also co-operated on the following: Aid under the non-quota section of the European Regional Development Fund: IR£16m was spent in border areas between 1980 and 1985 to develop tourism and craft industries.

This is the sole entry under the heading of cross-border cooperation, from a report which could be expected to stress this aspect of relations between Britain and Ireland.

The Hillsborough Agreement of 1985 did extend this aspect but not to any dramatic extent. Thus, when Britain prepared its submission to the EC outlining its economic policy intentions and seeking support from the Structural Funds in the context of 1992, it had little to say on this particular issue. An EC-assisted social, economic and environmental study of the northwest of Ireland was mentioned, as was cross-border cooperation in the area of higher education. The key paragraph reads rather blandly:

> Further opportunities for cross-border studies and co-operation may be forthcoming in the context of the development actions outlined in the preceding sections, and these will be considered on their merits and in the light of public expenditure priorities at the time.[13]

A number of other reports point to areas where industrial cooperation and integration could be pursued between the two economies. For example, Co-operation North has pointed to a range of activities, particularly involving small- and medium-sized enterprises, which could lead to joint ventures and an all-Ireland drive to increase innovation and technical expertise. The main point, however, is that very little of such activity has actually materialized. Though a joint proposal from the British and Dublin governments to a Community programme specifically intended to promote cross-border projects was made in 1991, indications are that the proposal is minimal in economic terms and it is certainly likely to have little if any political significance.

There is a certain economic analysis of Ireland which stresses the role of economic integration in leading to a political settlement. Thus, Paul Teague advocates as his preferred option 'some form of informal rolling economic integration, pursued on a case-by-case basis'. This would include the existing Border Area Development Plans and the author notes that: 'Of particular significance is the construction of a modern road-link between Belfast and Dublin. In no other European region is the road network between two major capitals so outmoded.'[14] This may be so, but it is hard to conceive of a motorway scheme as a major contribution to economic integration and this in turn as a giant step forward for peace and reconciliation. The project is so hemmed in by provisos – integration must be informal to avoid the 'political problems' which would arise from the more formal schemes – that it is rendered marginal even in its own terms.

The single market

In the 1980s economic performance in Western Europe was increasingly falling behind that in the US and Japan. The failure of the EC to actually achieve a common market was identified as a major reason for this. (Tariffs on trade between member states had often simply been replaced by other types of barriers.) The founding document of the EC, namely the Treaty of Rome, was amended by the Single European Act (SEA) of 1986. The main objectives of this Act were as follows:

- to set a date of the end of 1992 for the completion of the single market;
- to establish as a Community aim the strengthening of economic and social cohesion between member states;
- to give the Community powers in the area of research and technology;
- to incorporate the economic and monetary union, the European Monetary System and the European Currency Unit, into the Community's legal framework;
- to confirm the Community's responsibilities in the social policy area;
- to recognize the Community's powers in environmental protection; and
- to provide for cooperation between member states in foreign policy.[15]

Perhaps even more importantly, to facilitate the vastly accelerated decision making which was needed to achieve these objectives, majority decisions were allowed in a number of areas instead of the previously required unanimity of member states.

Carlo De Benedetti, the far-sighted head of Olivetti in Italy, has remarked that: '1992 is the only possible rational response to market globalisation and the growing competitiveness of the United States and Japan. Europe and its companies have no alternative. 1992 is a necessity.'[16] Whether Europe and its peoples will feel the same as the effects of 1992 unfold is another question. After the Single European Act had been passed, the so-called 'Cecchini Report' articulated the rationale for a single market in glowing terms:

The release of these constraints [on the achievement of a single market] will trigger a supply-side shock to the Community as a whole. The name of the shock is European market integration. Costs will come down. Prices will follow ... Ever present competition will ensure the completion of a self-sustaining virtuous circle.[17]

Instead of the vicious circle of underdevelopment, inflation, poverty and unemployment, we are presented with a new virtuous circle where lowered prices stimulate demand, in turn allowing European business to expand and meet competition on a global scale. Removing protective barriers in a bid to make European business more innovative and competitive with respect to its US and Japanese rivals has, of course, its costs. The road to market integration will, according to Cecchini, 'be paved with tough adjustments' and it will signal a definitive end to 'national soft options'.[18]

To partly offset this harsh scenario, the 1992 project has been given a social as well as an economic dimension. This, according to Jacques Delors, President of the Commission of the European Communities, 'must lead to a more unified Community . . . [having] enlarged the resources available for helping the long-term unemployed, youth unemployment and rural development, as well as the backward regions of the Community'.[19] With the Republic and Northern Ireland both being designated backward regions, it is important to investigate the relative prospects for both economic integration and its accompanying 'social dimension'.

The 1992 plan will, according to its supporters, produce a 7 per cent growth in Community output, a 5 per cent cut in prices and the creation of 5 million new jobs within six years. This projection is based on studies of the 'Cost of Non-Europe', that is to say, what would happen if integration does not occur. As an accurate forecast of what will happen, these studies leave much to be desired. Government action is a decisive variable which has not been considered: governments may or may not respond as rational economic actors should. Furthermore, this optimistic scenario is based on projections for the richer states and ignores the very different economies of Ireland, Portugal, Spain and Greece. However, it is not the precise accuracy of the 1992 studies which should concern us but their underlying rationale.

The new economic liberalism on a European scale is essentially about the intensification of competition. The two most important practical economic measures in this respect are the drive to open up public procurement and the integration of credit and finance. At present each government buys large quantities of goods and services from private companies, with these orders traditionally being channelled to domestic suppliers. Though military procurements are specifically excluded, competitive tendering across the EC will prevail after 1992 for all other areas of public procurement. The objective is to stop the disguised protection of home markets under the present system. In the financial sector, there is a similar move towards integration and liberalization. Money and credit systems will become interdependent across the EC as freedom of movement for banks, as well as capital, is established. In summary, the 1992 programme will accelerate economic integration in Western Europe and narrow the scope for autonomous national economic policies.

The objective of economic integration entails welding together the 12 EC states into a single market of 320 million people. To ensure that this market is an expanding one, the neo-liberal economists behind 1992 have prescribed a flexible market, where resources, be they human, material or financial, can flow into the areas of greatest economic advantage. The market integration programmes will thus lead to a process of national disintegration. This will occur at the level of finances because the free circulation of money and capital makes national credit policies almost impossible. It will also occur at the level of social relations, where any national class compromise will tend to be dissolved by the liberalization of capital flows. For workers, of course, flexibility often means speed-ups, unemployment and a general uncertainty about the future. This will be the case throughout the new, more open, EC unless the progressive political forces which have won various degrees of influence on the national level organize and act to win at least as much on the EC level.

Integration of the Western European economies will lead inevitably to concentration. As the Commission's own study of the future of the pharmaceutical industry makes clear: 'In the longer-term the effects of unifying the European market will be to make the strong stronger and the weak weaker.'[20] In the language of neo-liberalism, there will be winners and losers. The 1992 programme is explicitly intended to result in the liquidation of smaller firms dependent on their home market. There has already been a wave of merger activities in the lead-up to 1992, as is evident from the pages of the financial press. In Euro-speak, this is known as 'seizing the opportunity of 1992'. Or as the SDLP notes:

Although the European Market, 323 million consumers, will be open to Northern Ireland business, the Northern Ireland market will be just as open to European firms. The most efficient, most competitive companies will be the winners – those badly prepared will be the losers.[21]

Instead of questioning the logic of this scenario, however, the SDLP concludes that: 'The priority, therefore for Northern Ireland, is to ensure that its companies are prepared.' Unfortunately, this will not help the employees of companies which are liquidated, nor the regions which will suffer.

The Republic of Ireland will, according to some commentaries, stand to gain from the completion of the internal market. Government stockbrokers Bloxham Maguire are, however, less optimistic and conclude in their report that: 'The Irish economy could suffer all of the negative effects which are expected in the 1992 process by the EC Commission but very little of the benefits.'[22] The South's economy simply lacks the number of large-sized indigenous industrial firms capable of establishing themselves in an integrated European market. As the Economist Intelligence Unit predicts: 'The size of firm necessary to exploit the economies of scale created by the single market effectively excludes much of Irish industry . . . [which] will become dominated by giant industrial conglomerates capable of wiping out less efficient, smaller operations.'[23] The language of 'efficiency' spells rationalization and unemployment. For the big conglomerates referred to, Irish industries are seen as ripe for 'cherry-picking' where foreign-based businesses compete for the 'cherries', the particularly profitable areas of local industry.

For Northern Ireland also it is hard to find an optimistic reading of the prospects after 1992. For example, the opening up of the market for public procurement could be potentially more damaging in this region than elsewhere. Seventy per cent of employment in the North is dependent on public spending, compared with an EC average of around 40 per cent. Though labour costs are relatively low in the North, Portugal now offers labour costs three or four times lower, thus eliminating any comparative advantage in this respect. Even if the UK maintains its competitive position in a post-1992 Europe, and this is a big assumption, there is little reason to believe that benefits will 'trickle down' evenly into Northern Ireland. Finally, the squeeze on small businesses as concentration takes place will severely affect this sector, on which successive British governments have pinned so much hope.

Unequal development

Michael Besikofer of the EC's Social Affairs Department acknowledged at a recent conference that:

> There may be a number of serious regional problems arising from
> the restructuring process . . . Thus the impact of the Single Market
> may be much more severe for some of the regional areas, giving rise
> to an accentuation of certain existing regional disparities.

The overall prospect for the 'Western periphery' of the EC – basically
Ireland – after 1992 seems to be for a more accelerated development of
underdevelopment than would otherwise be the case. That is to say
development will take place but this will generally only accentuate the
peripheral and underdeveloped nature of the region.

Knowing that the creation of the single market would accentuate
regional inequalities, the Council of Ministers agreed in 1988 to
increase the Structural Funds (comprising the Regional Development
Fund, the Social Fund and the Agricultural Fund) from £5 billion in
1987 to £9 billion in 1992, producing an overall doubling of the Funds
by 1993. However, the Structural Funds still represent less than 0.2 per
cent of income generated in the EC. Furthermore, the increase in the
structural funds cannot compensate for the losses resulting from the
'reform' of the CAP as outlined in the subsequent section.

When he was Minister of Finance for the Republic, Ray McSharry
ruled out the possibility of increased payments from the Regional and
Social Funds being an adequate substitute for the revenue losses arising
from harmonization of indirect taxes. The Economist Intelligence Unit
notes that: 'Even if the transfers [of funds from the EC] are used
efficiently their impact is likely to be limited by their small size.'[24] In
the past, the Dublin government has tended to apply for a vast number
of investment projects to ensure a level of budgetary support for the
state, with little regard for the efficiency of the investment. Even an
optimistic forecast would only see EC transfers to the Republic
increasing by about 1–2 per cent per annum above the rate of inflation.
For Northern Ireland, there is considerable confusion as to the likely
impact of the single market. Thus, the SDLP can state that: 'Clearly
Northern Ireland stands to benefit from being part of a dynamic,
growing Europe which is on the move again,' yet a few paragraphs later
recognize that: 'It is difficult to know how Northern Ireland as a region
will fare under the Single Market.'[25] However, there is no reason to
expect Northern Ireland to escape the trend towards unequal development in peripheral regions.

While it is true that 1992 will open up markets in the core regions to the suppliers in the periphery, it will also open up the periphery to the usually more competitive suppliers based in the core. Being prepared for the common market may prove to be not enough, as suppliers in the core will be at least equally prepared. In the absence of changes to the underlying disadvantages of the peripheral regions, there is no particular reason to suppose that in general the suppliers in the periphery will be in a position to exploit the opportunities to their advantage. Reports prepared by the Northern Ireland Economic Council (NIEC) jointly with the National Economic and Social Council (NESC) in 1988 and by NESC alone in 1989 acknowledge this danger. The latter report in particular expresses serious misgivings that the Structural Funds are anything like adequate to counter tendencies for accentuating existing patterns of uneven development. Recently, Ireland, Portugal, Greece and, most effectively, Spain have attempted to link any increased integration of the EC with a more adequate regional policy. It remains to be seen whether an adequate EC regional policy will result from these efforts.

The border

We have already noted in the section above on cross-border cooperation that the British government's own regional plan for the North does not have much to say on the issue of the border. According to the SDLP: 'For Ireland in particular 1992 will mean the effective disappearance of the border for practical and commercial purposes.'[26] However, the border in Ireland in relation to 1992 is not only an economic or customs frontier. Certainly a customs post between Belfast and Dublin may be pointless, following the harmonization of VAT and excise duties after 1992. Yet, no one has seriously proposed that this means that the border will be dismantled. The Hillsborough Agreement of 1985 between the London and Dublin governments referred to cross-border cooperation primarily in the field of security. Cooperation between the security forces North and South was stepped up and the latter began to assume a much more central role in the struggle to contain the Republican insurgents in the North. The border may no longer pose a barrier to the extradition of political prisoners to the North, but again this is hardly the same as its fading away in a harmonious re-unification of Ireland.

Clearly, while present developments may diminish the importance of state borders within the EC, the member states will only cooperate within a framework which accepts their existing territorial integrity. Some political forces in Ireland –primarily the SDLP but also the major parties in the South –have occasionally hinted that the political changes which they believe will develop from the present period of major reform in the EC will fundamentally alter the existing patterns of sovereignty in Ireland. Perhaps this is so, but in 15 years of participation in European politics these same political leaders have rarely raised the issue of partition and Britain's presence in Ireland in the various Community institutions. Any changes in sovereignty will have a long and complex evolution and there is no guarantee that the final outcome will provide the people of Ireland with greater control of their own destiny. It is thus somewhat unrealistic to expect the disappearance of customs checks to lead to the disappearance of the border, partition and the continued role of Britain in Irish politics. Nor will the historical weight of underdevelopment in the border areas be overcome by the liberalization of trade in 1992 –on the contrary, we can expect higher than average unemployment and emigration rates to be perpetuated and, indeed, accentuated as the cold winds of international free-trade politics hit Ireland.

By the early 1980s, considerable pressure had built up for a reform of the CAP, mainly as a response to the costs involved in maintaining the high-price policies of the CAP and the related problems of overproduction. The introduction of milk quotas in 1984 was the first serious step in that direction. But the problem is far from being solved. To keep production in line with quotas, farmers initially reacted with less intensive feeding, thereby adopting cost-effective methods of less output per cow. Soon, however, a return to intensive feeding put new pressure on the small dairy farmers to sell their quotas and to enter other, less profitable, farming areas. Equally sheep farming, which has traditionally been of particular importance in some of Northern Ireland's Less Favoured Areas, no longer provides a viable alternative for small farmers. Numbers of sheep in Northern Ireland doubled during the past decade and sheep meat is now approaching sufficiency level in the EC. This will inevitably lead to either a reduction in headage payments, which form a substantial part of income to many marginal farmers, or the regular application of quotas to sheep production.

Both support-prices and headage payments have favoured the larger farmers against the smaller ones as they are linked to output. Today, it is widely accepted that the CAP has failed both in providing adequate incomes to the smaller farmers and in promoting genuine rural development. Increasingly, a greater emphasis (in rhetorical terms at least) is being put on Integrated Rural Development, which should entail a coordinated programme of supportive measures which go beyond just agriculture. However, when we read the regional development plans prepared by the various governments to meet these objectives, we discover that little of substance is in fact under way or even seriously planned. Thus, the British government's 1989–93 plan for the North makes little mention of Integrated Rural Development, nor does it consider the way in which Community involvement could assist a rural development programme. In fact, the draft plan simply accepted the status quo:

> While there is a general acceptance of the CAP amongst the farming community in Northern Ireland it is clear that continuing price restraint, the introduction of stabilisers, the tightening of intervention arrangements and the drive towards a more market-oriented economy is likely to hit farmers' incomes in Northern Ireland proportionately more than in GB and in other areas where there is a greater spread of products and more opportunity for diversification.[27]

The EC has accepted that farmers in Northern Ireland do have particular problems and treats the region separately from Britain in many respects, but this remains of limited significance since the Commission of the European Community is ultimately subordinate to the member state governments in most policy areas. For example, the Maher Plan, calling for an integrated rural development in Northern Ireland and outlining detailed programmes for some of the most disadvantaged areas, was fully endorsed by the Commission in 1986, but in its implementation it relies on the goodwill of the British government which has shelved it indefinitely. It was only after considerable pressure had been applied by both the Commission and local interests that the Northern Ireland authorities announced measures specifically aimed at rural development. The likely effectiveness of these measures remains unclear.

Any major reform of the CAP threatens to reverse the relatively favoured treatment of the farming sector in the Republic. Agriculture is considerably more important in the South in terms of contribution to the economy and employment, so the impact of any reform will be greater. The reduction of the milk quota also has a knock-on effect on beef production, in that fewer dairy cows are necessary to produce the quota. This, as the Economist Intelligence Unit notes: 'Is especially serious as beef represents the only significant source of potential output growth in Irish agriculture over the next five years.'[28] The South's food industry will also become more concentrated as success in exporting will lead to the promotion of branded products. As in industry then, agriculture will see a process of concentration and a social decimation after 1992. The Border Areas Special Programme, including EC-assisted support for these areas, cannot change this fundamental conclusion.

Women

The impact of 1992 on women in Ireland will be considerable. Firstly, as Hazel Morrissey notes:

> Well-educated women from both parts of Ireland could have tremendous opportunities with Europe particularly if they have language training. Professional and business women could also gain from the moves towards harmonisation, where qualifications are recognised in all the member states without the need for additional retraining.[29]

Realistically, of course, this scenario will only be relevant to a small proportion of working women. For the majority, the term 'flexibility', which is at the very core of the 1992 project, will spell de-skilling and casualization. New technology, in particular, will increase the demand for a more flexible labour force.

Morrissey's report on women in 1992 also notes that:

> Unemployment by occupation reveals that the highest concentration of female unemployed are to be found in clerical workers, shop assistants, domestic and personal services, and textiles. It is these kind of jobs which will become more vulnerable after 1992 both in terms of new technology and declining manufacture.[30]

Restructuring of the European economies after 1992 will lead to rationalization and redundancies. The decline of manufacturing, particularly in Northern Ireland, is unlikely to be matched by an increase of services, in what is already largely a service economy. New technology, which is central to 1992, could also severely affect the position of working women. These are the realities of 1992, which cannot be disguised by the EC's stated commitment to the full implementation of equal pay and equal treatment of men and women.

Moreover, the British and Irish governments seem set to resist even the limited progressive content of EC legislation regarding women. Thus, the Equal Treatments Directive, passed by the EC in 1976, was not incorporated into British legislation until 1986 and only implemented in Northern Ireland in 1988.

Britain, characteristically, wanted to see small firms exempted from the equal-pay legislation, in spite of the well-known fact that a large proportion of women work in this sector. The Republic, likewise, has simply ignored EC rulings. The Southern trade unions are still calling for the Dublin government to introduce legislation bringing the state into line with a 1982 directive on part-time work. We thus have a situation where the member states are prepared to enable the EC to implement wide-ranging changes which have serious (if often indirect) negative effects on women's rights while the same member states simply do not implement more limited direct EC measures to enhance women's rights. Whereas a small minority of women stand to benefit from 1992, the vast majority will not see any improvement.

This pattern of selective commitment to the EC, its policies and its authority by the member states is not confined to women's issues. Indeed, appreciation of the precise nature of the political relationship between the Community institutions and the member states is of central importance to any analysis of present developments.

The social dimension

The proponents of 1992 lay considerable emphasis on the fact that the economic project also has a benign social dimension. Reading between the lines of the influential Cecchini report, however, one obtains a less favourable impression. There we are told that: 'Restructuring entire sectors, shifts in employment, new demands on labour mobility and training, the regional distribution of new wealth – these are so many factors whose adjustment to the new market conditions carries their own social and political costs.'[31] This frank evaluation of the social costs of 1992 must frame any consideration of the so-called social dimension.

The EC projects the following for 1992:

- health and safety at work initiatives;
- special support for disadvantaged groups;

- additional training;
- moves to harmonize key working conditions; and
- increased discussion between trade unions and employers.

Potentially, there is indeed a reformist impulse behind these measures and EC President Delors has recently promised far reaching reforms to the European Confederation of Trade Unions. Yet all assessments of the likely impact of 1992 on trade unionists in Ireland are negative. Ireland as a whole appears scheduled for a role as a labour reserve to the advanced industrial core of post-1992 Europe. The Economist Intelligence Unit notes that: 'One key factor in this is the relatively low cost and low mobility of staff. Good quality computer science graduates can be employed in Ireland for little more than half of their cost in the USA.'[32] Emigration from the Republic is projected to average 25,000 per annum and even with that drain there will be over 306,000 unemployed by 1992. After 1992, the much wanted 'freedom of movement' for people as much as money would seem to mean the 'freedom' for Irish people to choose emigration rather than the dole queue.

There is, in brief, no prospect of a Europe-wide super Keynesian welfare state being provided to sweeten the economic pill of 1992. As O'Siochru writes in an evaluation of the implications of 1992 for the Irish trade unions:

> Behind the Social Dimension is the conviction of the Commission and the Council of Ministers [or at least most of them] that in order to accomplish the transition to 1992, with its attendant restructuring and dislocation, some form of organised co-operation is needed between capital and organised labour, 'social' dialogue.[33]

From this point of view, the social dimension is clearly not primarily motivated by concerns of equity.

The current Maastricht project of a European supra-national state builds on the inevitable economic consequences of completing the single market. The 1992 programme will transfer most of the policy instruments whereby nation states have hitherto implemented industrial policies to the EC level. The inescapable conclusion is that national industrial policies will, after 1992, become virtually impossible. Individual states seem prepared to surrender their traditional mechanisms of intervention, protectionism and regulation used in the past to build up a viable national industry. At the same time it can be argued that national industrial policies are becoming increasingly impotent in any case. As a recent study concludes 'the alternative of relying completely on national parliaments to secure democratic government is increasingly dangerous and unreliable because of economic internationalisation which threatens to move huge areas of national life beyond national control.'[34] Faced with this reality it appears that any democratic alternative must entail a strategy which, while recognizing the continuing power and relevance of the nation state, is capable of also going beyond narrow national boundaries and engaging with energy and effectiveness on the international level. Any strategy which does not have an international dimension that goes beyond general platitudes of solidarity is simply inadequate.

Just as the issue of economic sovereignty is more complex that it might appear at first, so too is the issue of political sovereignty. The moves towards a more integrated EC have certainly involved the transfer of a measure of political sovereignty to the Community level. However, it need hardly be pointed out that the nature of political sovereignty in Northern Ireland is a contentious and unresolved issue. Moreover, in the Republic military neutrality is frequently due to marginality rather than principled commitment. The military implications of future developments in a more integrated EC is far from clear. Tensions which already existed within NATO have been exacerbated by the collapse of state socialism in Eastern Europe. Larger states such as Germany, Italy and Spain appear to be shifting towards the more independent position already adopted by France. Britain and the Netherlands, on the other hand, seem to be in favour of the US continuing to play its predominant role. An argument can certainly be made that a more active, non-aligned intervention on military issues might be particularly justifiable and effective during the present period of profound change. Active efforts to promote de-militarization would also be more honest than any isolationist and marginalized stance which clings to the rhetoric of neutrality due to convenience rather than commitment.

Conclusion

If the targets set by the EC for the end of 1992 are met then Europe will be simply transformed. Even if all these ambitions are not achieved the

European economy has already been influenced to develop in ways in which it otherwise would not have done. Some overall economic growth is likely to come about due to increased economic efficiency. However, the benefits of this are going to be distributed extremely unevenly unless major political developments take place. The weaker regions and economic groups within the EC are likely to come under more pressure from the stronger. Increased competition will produce downward pressure on wage levels and more business failures will arise.

There are some signs that political forces are beginning to muster to counter such tendencies. Ireland, Spain, Portugal and Greece are becoming more outspoken in their opposition to developments which result in greater pressures being put on their national economies without adequate mechanisms to counter such outcomes also being developed. It must be acknowledged, however, that this political battle has only started and will have a genuine chance of success only if progressive political forces effectively coordinate their efforts to develop a social dimension to the new Europe and address forcefully the so-called 'democratic deficit' in EC workings.

A final argument for the need for critical political engagement in this exercise is the fact that it may offer the only viable mechanism for Irish people to counter international economic trends which so often act to their disadvantage. National economic and political balances of power will in future increasingly be established within the wider framework of the EC. It is becoming less and less appropriate to rely exclusively on national mechanisms to secure a democratic future.

7

Alternative Scenarios

(With Douglas Hamilton)

Previous chapters have looked in some detail at the various political and social factors which have shaped the development of the Irish economy North and South. This chapter takes the discussion one step further and outlines the range of possible scenarios that could be envisaged for the future political and economic development of Ireland. As will be seen, some of the scenarios will be considered more likely than others and in the context of this book more desirable. It is the intention, however, to argue that only one of these possibilities, namely the Democratic Economy option, can even begin to solve the deeprooted problems, political, social and economic, that have plagued Ireland this century. We believe that it is important that the likely consequences of these various scenarios should be clearly spelt out so that the policy options so frequently put forward by politicians and economic commentators can be fully understood.

An important argument of this book is that the partition of Ireland, and as a result the direct and indirect dependency of the economy North and South on external forces, has been the greatest impediment to the development of Ireland during this century. Therefore, we believe that the various paths that can be envisaged for the future development of Ireland can be divided between those which maintain the partition of Ireland, and those which lead towards reunification. Accordingly this chapter is divided, for the purposes of both presentation and under- standing, into five different scenarios which follow one of these two paths. It could be argued that in so doing we exclude some possible outcomes or through presentation belittle the arguments for other solutions. It should be clear, however, that it is not our intention to put forward what some would term a neutral analysis, but which in reality

135

adds up to nothing more than the well-worn arguments in defence of the clearly failed status quo. We simply state what we believe to be a number of logical policy responses to the analysis which we have presented.

The five scenarios to be discussed are as follow:

1. continuation of the status quo;
2. some form of devolved government in Northern Ireland or, at the extreme, complete independence and separation;
3. positions revolving around the concept of economic harmonization;
4. the reunification of Ireland within a capitalist framework and;
5. the reunification of Ireland within a radical democratic framework.

More of the same

This scenario is, of course, that which has been pursued in the North since direct rule from London was introduced in 1972. Previous chapters have discussed how Ireland has reached its current stage of development (or underdevelopment). In the North of Ireland, Britain has ruled over an area which has never experienced anything other than economic disadvantage compared with much of the rest of Western Europe. Indeed, historian Joe Lee has described the Northern economy as one that 'counts among the striking economic failures of the century'.[1] This despite a subvention from the British government which in 1990 totalled around £2bn, that being the difference between what is raised from taxation in the North and what is actually spent by government. Without this level of subvention Bob Rowthorn has suggested that 'Northern Ireland is now on a par with middle-range Latin American countries like Argentina and Chile. It is in, effect an underdeveloped country kept afloat by subsidies from the UK.'[2] The economic failure of the South has also been amply described with Raymond Crotty pointing out that:

> almost half those born and surviving childhood have emigrated from Ireland since 1871 . . . the rate at which people have emigrated has hardly changed since the country became independent in 1922. Net

emigration between 1911, the last pre-independence census year, and 1961 was 45 per cent of the number of births registered.[3]

Moreover he goes on to say that 'less than half as many people get a livelihood in the Republic now as did so 140 years ago; fewer get a livelihood there now than when the country became independent'.

Given this background there is little reason to expect a significantly improved economic performance in the future. If we were to forecast merely on the basis of past trends then clearly only the most optimistic British or Irish minister would expect significant improvement. Indeed Roper and Gudgin[4] of the Northern Ireland Economic Research Centre (NIERC) forecast employment and GDP in the North to grow at a slower rate than in the UK economy. And this against a growth rate in the UK which is, and is forecast to continue to be, significantly below that experienced in the rest of Western Europe until the end of this century. In the South the Economic and Social Research Institute forecasts a rate of growth in the economy far below that necessary to resolve the chronic problems in the labour market of low employment, high unemployment and the continuing haemorrhage of emigration.[5] This pessimistic view is mirrored by that taken by the National Economic and Social Council which expects the general standard of living in the South to diverge further from the European Community's average as a result of the creation of the single European market.[6]

As we have seen, however, many initiatives, both political and economic, have been introduced in Ireland with the aim of increasing economic growth. In the North, after decades of high and largely automatic levels of subsidization of industry in the form of unconditional grants, recent reports from independent bodies, in particular the Northern Ireland Economic Council (NIEC) and the NIERC, have shown that it has been all to no avail. In the case of the NIEC's analysis less than 10,000 jobs assisted by the IDB were still in place after six years, only 40 per cent of the jobs planned for, and at a cost of over £600m.[7] Gudgin et al. of the NIERC point out that 'only 65 firms employing 16,000 people remain to show (in 1986) for all the effort of industrial attraction from 1945 to 1973'.[8] Recent studies of the level of productivity in Northern Ireland compared with other areas also suggest that despite a high level of industrial assistance little improvement has been forthcoming.[9] Moreover, the NIEC has pointed out that during the 1980s manufacturing employment in the North declined by 42,000 at a time when 'the two development agencies, the IDB and LEDU, spent over £1bn on industrial development and claimed to have promoted

over 74,000 jobs and renewed or maintained a further 100,000 jobs'.[10]
This research adds up to a damning indictment of the effectiveness of
industrial policy in Northern Ireland.

A common feature of all these studies is their failure to ask where
such large amounts of public money went if they did not go towards the
expansion of manufacturing employment. The much commented upon
high number of luxury cars and flamboyant lifestyles of a significant
number of people in the North would appear to provide much of the
answer. Indeed McGregor and Borooah have shown that the distribution
of income in the North of Ireland is more unequal than in Britain,[11]
which tends to give some confirmation of the way in which public
money has been abused. Indeed it might be that it is only by viewing
industrial policy in this way that the contradiction between the
apparently significant number of successful business persons in the
North of Ireland and the small number of successful companies can be
understood.

The past failures of industrial policy in the North have only recently
been recognized by the British government, although rarely publicly
admitted to, and as a result a new so-called economic strategy was
introduced in 1990 called 'Competing in the 1990s'. The basis of this
strategy is that industry in the North has to be more competitive if it is
to succeed and when this occurs employment will automatically be
created. Consequently it is intended that in the future assistance to
industry will only be granted when firms show signs that they intend to
improve their competitive position. This, of course, begs the question
of what criteria were used in the past to assess the worthiness of
industrial projects. More importantly, however, it reflects the belated
introduction into the North of Ireland of a more 'Thatcherite' industrial
policy (although it should be stressed that the overall budget for
industrial policy continues to be increased). The confusing way in
which the new policy was introduced and the clear problems which the
development agencies had in trying to cope with it suggest a very low
level of confidence for future improvement. This was demonstrated by
the fact that while the new policy was focused around the concept of
competitiveness, the IDB issued a document requesting interested
bodies to submit views on how competitiveness should be defined. In
other words a new strategy was launched in which the main concept
was not defined. In summary this hardly adds up to the stable and
confidence-building base required for the effective implementation of
industrial policy.

Meanwhile in the South the development of consensus politics continues. A high priority is now given to the involvement of the so-called social partners (trade unions, business and farmers) in the formulation of overall economic policy for the state. With the expiry in 1990 of the first real attempt at consensus politics, the 'Programme for National Recovery', the more recent 'Programme for Economic and Social Progress' is to run for the duration of the 1990s. The basis of these approaches is that agreement is reached across a range of issues in society such as the health service, education, social welfare and of course the economy, including employment. The major ingredient in this is agreement on the rate of pay increases that are to be made in future years.

It is undoubtedly true that a fair degree of consensus has been achieved, although some political parties (in particular the Labour Party) have felt aggrieved by their exclusion from major policy making until recently. The effect of this approach on the economy is rather more ambiguous. While some would argue that improvements to the Southern economy were made in the late 1980s, it is clear that major improvements in the key indicators, notably employment, unemployment and emigration, have not been forthcoming. The uncertain times ahead, and indeed the less than challenging targets set for employment creation, suggest that an insufficient number of jobs will be created to offset the high levels of unemployment and involuntary emigration. In other words, the key problems of the Southern Irish economy will remain unresolved and, as in the North, the success of industrial policy is highly questionable.

In future the role for government in the South is to be much more limited than in the past, and is simply to create the 'right' conditions from which growth in the economy will arise. Des O'Malley, the Minister for Industry and Commerce, stated at the end of 1990 in his department's review of industrial performance that 'it is clear that a poor correlation exists between State expenditure (direct and tax-related) on industry and net employment creation'.[12] Furthermore he went to say, 'I do not subscribe to the view that the industrial development agencies "create jobs" in industry.' The increasingly arms-length or what has become know as the 'climatological' approach to industry looks likely to be pursued in the 1990s. Given the appalling poor performance of indigenous Irish industry, as analyzed at length in the recent Culliton Report, since the formation of the state it is difficult to expect much improvement, especially in an environment in which government is to take such a backroom role.

Devolution in the North

In contrast to the other four scenarios presented in this chapter this section considers possible political arrangements set solely within the North of Ireland. These are some form of devolved government in Northern Ireland, similar to that which existed for most of the period since the partition of Ireland, or full independence and separation of the six counties from both Britain and the rest of Ireland. A third option which has on occasion been considered elsewhere, the repartitioning of Ireland, is not discussed here. Although some would argue that this is a future possibility its economic significance would only be an extension of arguments and analysis we present in this chapter.

Between 1922 and 1972 when direct rule from London was established, Northern Ireland had its own devolved government. The Stormont government, although directly accountable to Westminster, maintained a degree of autonomy over the policies adopted towards, among other areas, local industry. Although macroeconomic policy on such matters as taxation, monetary and exchange-rate policy were implemented at the British level, policies towards industry were effectively determined locally. In many ways these policies, as we discussed in Chapter 3, were similar to those which have been pursued through direct rule over the past 20 years. However, a major characteristic of economic policies pursued either by Stormont or London has been the extremely high level of financial assistance available for the development of the local economy in comparison with other areas of Britain. In other words, although nominally operating much the same political structures as the rest of Britain, the actual implementation of economic policy in the North of Ireland has, at least in magnitude, been quite different under direct rule. Therefore, the legacy of the Stormont government continues to the present day.

The respective positions of the political parties in the North towards a return of a devolved government are, to say the least, difficult to ascertain, with respect to both nationalist and unionist parties. Only the Workers' Party and the Alliance Party are clearly in favour of some form of devolution (also, it should be said, is the majority of the population in the North if some opinion polls are to be believed). The basic political argument for devolved government, put very simply, is that power should be placed as much as possible in the hands of local people so that policies are implemented and issues resolved at the local level. It is in this context that both democracy and accountability are extended from that existing under direct rule, and that greater local knowledge and expertise are utilized for the effective resolution of problems. From the policy point of view, of course, it would mean that policies could be designed which were more specifically appropriate for the problems of the North of Ireland. On the economic front, for example, it is often argued by trade unionists in the North that the policies pursued at the British level are designed to tackle problems in the southeast or some other region of England which are quite different from those in the North of Ireland. We have already argued that the economies in the North and South of Ireland have more in common with each other than either do with Britain. In this sense, therefore, the political and economic arguments for devolution would appear incontestable. The experience of devolution in the North of Ireland, of course, tells us something quite different since it was the sectarian policies implemented by local politicians in Stormont which led to the imposition of direct rule in 1972.

Apart from the political arguments presented above, the economics of a devolved government in the North of Ireland are rarely put. This is in contrast to the situation in Scotland which has long had a movement pushing for devolution and has on various occasions attempted to formulate the policies which could be pursued by a Scottish parliament, and what their effect would be. Much of that discussion concentrates on the extent of tax raising powers which would be allowed in Scotland since this would determine the resources to enable autonomous policy making. Despite this more detailed discussion, however, the basic arguments in favour of devolution in Scotland remain political and not economic in nature. In the North of Ireland this is also the case although the political case is made more problematic by the deep split in the sentiments and allegiances of the population compared with the more homogeneous block in Scotland. In other words the past experience of autonomous policy making by the unionist majority in the North during the period of the Stormont government, in terms of sectarianism and the political problems that it led to, undermines political arguments for devolution. It is difficult to believe that devolving power to the unionist majority in the North of Ireland would lead to an alleviation of economic and social problems in nationalist areas. Indeed, previous experience would suggest that quite the opposite would be more likely.

A more extreme extension of devolution would be the establishment of a completely independent and separate state for the North of Ireland. Although such proposals have been put forward in the past, in particular by Liam de Paor[13] and political organizations like the UDA, we do not believe it is worth dwelling too long on such a scenario. This is because the economic viability of a state comprising of just 1.5 million people, and which is deeply divided politically, is highly questionable. In short such a state would not have the resources, whether natural or financial, to maintain anything like the current standard of living. Indeed without the British subvention an independent state in the North of Ireland would simply collapse.

It is, however, worth looking briefly at one economic issue which has been related to this scenario. This is the contention that the unemployment problem in the North of Ireland could be ameliorated if the level of wages were allowed to reduce the cost of labour. This argument, or some variant of it such as a rate of increase in money wages needing to be less than that pertaining at the British level, has been given prominence by economists such as Norman Gibson and Tom Wilson.[14] Put simply they argue that the market for labour is not being allowed to operate freely enough because of obstructive factors such as trade unions and levels of social security which keep wage rates above what the market would determine. Therefore they argue that wages should be allowed to drop or at least not rise as quickly as in Britain, thereby lowering the cost of labour and increasing the level of employment. This, of course, is simply the restatement of classical economics which states that economies will inevitably reach a full employment equilibrium if labour markets are allowed to operate freely. The argument against this position, which many thought Keynes had buried for good, is simply that the main determinant of employment is not the level of money wages but the level of effective demand in the economy. Only with sufficient demand in an economy can full employment be achieved. If, as the classical economists suggest, wages are encouraged to fall at a time of unemployment then this will lead to a drop in effective demand, a fall in output and a subsequent fall in employment. The end result is even higher unemployment that before. Therefore, apart from the economic and social costs of such a policy for individuals who would receive lower wages and therefore less spending power, the overall effect of such a policy in the case of an already deeply depressed regional economy such as the North of Ireland, where wages are already relatively low, is completely misguided.

To summarize this section, a devolved government in the North of Ireland could lead to the implementation of more appropriate policies for the economy which in turn could lead to limited improvements. But the clear risk is that the autonomy in policy making provided by devolution would allow the return of the more blatantly sectarian policies of the past. A completely separate and independent state for the six counties of the North of Ireland is simply unviable, even more so than the present state with its financial and economic link to Britain. This, of course, returns us to our previous arguments which stated that economic solutions cannot be found within political structures internal to Northern Ireland.

Economic harmonization

This scenario is proposed by a number of protagonists including the British Labour Party, the SDLP, some newspapers and trade unions and, significantly, in a 1992 speech by George Quigley, chair of the Ulster Bank and of the Institute of Directors in Northern Ireland. The key focus of this approach is the development of increased economic cooperation between the North and South of Ireland. This approach is also closely linked to developments taking place within Europe, and, in particular, the elimination of non-tariff barriers between member states of the EC and the creation of a single European market as discussed in Chapter 6.

In essence this approach argues, at least in terms of its economic aspects, for what the British Labour Party in its policy statement in 1988 'Towards a United Ireland' called reform and harmonization. In particular, a long-term strategy is urged 'based on the strengthening of economic ties with the Republic and on developing cross-border initiatives of benefit to both parts of the island'. Also 'joint approaches to the EC for special assistance' would be made 'linked to a programme of economic harmonization and joint development programmes'. Such cooperation on the economic front is part of a wider multi-dimensional policy of cooperation on other institutional, cultural, legal and security aspects and is seen as a crucial component of the overriding political objective of achieving a united Ireland without violating the so-called principle of consent. The harmonization of the institutions and policies of 'the two parts of Ireland promotes reform and facilitates the material, political and cultural conditions essential for successful unification'. In this sense, policies of economic cooperation recognize that the economies North and South have much more in common than they do with Britain and that, therefore, only all-Ireland initiatives will have a full and positive effect. In particular, policies dealing with the issues of monetary reform, industrial strategy, agriculture, energy, transport and tourism would be furthered. An important part of the strategy will be movement towards a common currency. On the institutional front all-Ireland bodies for industrial development, tourism and energy would be established immediately, and a common approach towards regional development and, in particular, in relation to the EC. The economic rationale for such moves is recognized as not just the commonality of the economies North and South but also the diseconomies created by partition.

In general, in this scenario all-Ireland economic policies are seen as a key component of the overriding political objective of reunification. The evolutionary methods of persuasion and beneficial experience will be furthered rather than that of force or imposition. While this may be theoretically plausible, and indeed desirable, one crucial criticism of the approach still remains. This is that, despite the rhetoric, reunification cannot be achieved because this approach continues to provide the unionist majority in the North with a veto over the process. In other words, the tangible benefits which would undoubtedly arise from all-Ireland policies towards the economy would be to no avail if the political preference of the unionist majority in the North (but minority in the whole of Ireland), demanded the continuation of British rule. So policies designed to benefit the whole of Ireland could, and in all probability would, be stopped by a minority of the population of Ireland.

While the unity by consent approach holds many commendable features it fails seriously because it is based ultimately on an undemocratic premise – one which derives from the partition of Ireland in 1922. By devising a strategy based on the partitionist framework the economic harmonization approach attempts the impossible. Ultimately the internal contradictions of such an approach would make it collapse. Although we have argued that the unity by consent approach is unworkable as a *political* strategy it is still worthwhile to look in more detail at some of the *economic* issues which arise from partition and some of the benefits which could arise from a reunited Ireland. The next scenario is, therefore, to a large extent a logical extension of what has been discussed in this section.

Capitalist united Ireland

Most debate among nationalists is based naturally enough on how to achieve a reunited Ireland and it is taken for granted that the political aims of reunification are sufficient grounds by themselves. What has not been discussed systematically, however, are the economic aspects of a reunited Ireland. One major exception to this was the various reports and submissions which were put forward as part of the New Ireland Forum in 1984. Most of what was submitted came from neo-classical economists such as Norman Gibson and Dermot McAleese and was quite restrictive in its analysis. Matters were viewed in purely economic terms, without acknowledging the wider political environment in which economic decisions are made. Despite this severe limitation, however, these submissions did highlight some of the economic benefits that would arise from a reunified Ireland which continued to be based on capitalist relations of production. The following paragraphs attempt to summarize the economic arguments put forward at the time of the New Ireland Forum and some more recent thinking which relates to the economics of partition.

Firstly, there is the important argument that partition reduced artificially the size of the home markets North and South. Put simply the domestic market in the South would increase by almost 50 per cent and in the North it would be more than trebled if Ireland were to be reunited. Given the importance of the size of home markets in determining future economic development it can be argued that partition significantly reduces the potential for the Irish economies. Turning the argument the other way around a reunited Ireland would create significant economic opportunities. Supporting this argument is the fact that a relatively large and dynamic home market is a necessary (though not sufficient) condition for firms to grow to a size whereby they can compete in international markets. This becomes all the more important the smaller the size of the domestic market and the degree of openness of the economy. A large domestic market can provide a relatively sheltered environment from competition from outside, generate rivalry domestically between indigenous firms and allow for the exploitation of economies of scale. Related to this discussion of the economics of a reunited Ireland is, of course, the impact of the creation of a single European market. However, as we discussed in Chapter 6, there are a number of issues associated with such a development, many of which are far from positive for Ireland.

What has occurred in Ireland, as we have shown in Chapters 2 and 3, is that not only are there two quite separate economies North and South but there are also dual economies *within* the two jurisdictions. On the first point, partition has clearly led to a situation of very low cross-border trade. This is low not just in terms of partition itself, but also in comparison with levels of trade which take place for example between similar sized economies in the Benelux area. In other words, the level of cross-border trade in Ireland is even lower than might have been expected. On the second point, as we have noted, the Irish economies North and South have been highly dependent on the attraction of external investment by transnational corporations. While the South continues to be successful at this, at least in terms of attracting a significant number of branch plants, the ultimate economic effect has not been maximized because linkages have not been developed between the externally owned and indigenous sectors. Therefore, a slow-growing indigenous sector, which has not been able to develop fully because of the small size and, therefore, less sophisticated type of demand in the domestic market, has been accompanied by a relatively faster-growing externally owned sector but whose wealth or surplus creation has been merely exported. This is reflected in the large outward flows of capital from the South which in 1990 totalled over £2.2bn and 10 per cent of GNP. In other words, that part of the economy which is actually growing and generating comparatively high levels of economic surplus has not reinvested it for the benefit of the Southern Irish economy. Indeed, such an outcome in terms of transfer pricing[15] and profit expatriation has been actively supported and encouraged by the generous, or more accurately non-existent, tax policies pursued by successive Southern governments.

A related set of arguments in terms of Irish underdevelopment and partition is that which emphasizes the economies of scope that can be generated from the clustering of firms and industries within geographically small areas. Regions in Germany and Italy show how dynamic and cumulatively virtuous economic linkages can be developed between a large number of small- to medium-sized firms in particular industries.

However, in the case of Ireland the small size of the domestic market and the low or primitive base from which such a development would have to start from would not favour this type of activity, at least in the absence of concerted action by government. Again this type of development would be much more feasible in a reunited and, therefore, larger domestic market.

It needs to be emphasized that while partition has burdened the Irish economy with significant costs, even a reunited Ireland would face immense economic difficulties because of its relatively small size, peripheral location and its underdevelopment due to its damaging dependence on external forces, whether it be the British economy and rule, transnational corporations or more recently the EC. In other words, partition has merely added to the problems which Ireland would in any case need to confront when competing in international capitalist markets. Indeed, in recognition of this the 'structuralist' approach put forward by Eoin O'Malley argues that latecomers to industrial develop-ment such as Ireland face huge barriers to entry into international markets, because of the inability of private industry to grow to a size sufficient to overcome the high development costs of entering and subsequently competing successfully against international firms. As O'Malley writes:

> Such barriers to entry exist in the wide range of industries characterised by factors such as economies of scale, large capital requirements, product differentiation, advanced technology, spe-cialised skills or dependence on the external economies inherent in large advanced industrial centres.[16]

To some extent, the structuralist approach is merely an extension of the debate over size already discussed above, but it goes further by implicitly recognizing the failure of traditional policies which aim to tackle the conventionally understood constraints on industrial develop-ment such as a lack of entrepreneurship, a lack of capital, an insufficient physical infrastructure and a low-quality labour force. A key aspect of the structuralist approach is that the policy response which flows from its analysis suggests a highly interventionist and multidimensional approach towards the development of pre-selected industries and firms with resources being highly concentrated.

Other aspects of the economics of partition include the profound underdevelopment of border areas. Because of the artificial division created by partition, areas which would have developed along natural

economic boundaries, rather than that determined by the border, have
not been able to develop normal trading relations. This can be seen most
clearly in those relatively populated areas along the border such as
Derry, Dundalk and Newry. It is clearly no coincidence that the border
areas both North and South are among the most disadvantaged in
Ireland. Indeed for most areas along the border there is hardly any
normal economic activity at all. Of course in the North this position has
been exacerbated by the deliberate underdevelopment of nationalist
areas through discrimination and neglect on the part of successive
British governments.

   A further aspect which was touched upon in the previous section is
the uncoordinated and uneconomic approach to almost all parts of
government policy such as industrial development, health services,
tourism, energy and transport. In these areas a significant degree of
duplication has taken place at high financial and public cost. This is
seen for example in the case of hospitals being built on either side of
the border by both the British and Irish governments when one hospital
would be much more sensible and economic. In this way Ireland has
been deprived of an integrated approach towards the provision of public
services. In addition the North has suffered from policies which have
been determined primarily by reference to what is deemed correct for
Britain and not by reference to the North's particular needs. It should
be noted in this context that the exceptional circumstances of the North
have allowed some degree of autonomy and differences from British
policy to be adopted and implemented. The benefits of this, however,
are doubtful since that autonomy, as we have discussed earlier in this
chapter, has been the very factor which has allowed sectarian policies
to be pursued.

   In conclusion, we would argue that while many tangible economic
benefits would, or at least could, arise from a reunited Ireland these are
limited and far from sufficient to resolve the deeprooted problems of
the Irish economy. It is to how these can be effectively tackled through
a more radical alternative that our attention now turns.

A democratic economy

Having examined the limitations of the united Ireland option under
existing social and political conditions we are obliged to present an
alternative which could point us towards a democratic economy. One

option, pursued by Kieran Allen in a critique of the notion that the Southern economy is still a neo-colony, is to argue that 'The fight is for a workers republic and international socialism, not an Éire Nua.'[17] The assumption is that calls for national economic development and 'economic sovereignty' are simply reactionary. The issue is seen to be not British neo-colonialism but 'world capitalism'. The problem with this perspective is that it simply takes us from fuzzy nationalist economics to abstract socialist economics. The notion of 'economic sovereignty' is certainly not viable if taken literally, given Ireland's close integration with the capitalist world economy. But this does not invalidate the aspirations to an all-Ireland national democracy where people may begin to exercise some accountability over the economy. The notion of dependent development (presented in Chapter 1) may help us break away from a sterile counterposition of outdated nationalist economics reminiscent of the 1930s and utopian calls for world revolution in a country which still has not completed its national democratic revolution.

One of the problems with dependency theory was that it did not clearly articulate what path non-dependent development might take beyond vague gestures about de-linking from the world economy. A policy of autarky – basically closing economic frontiers and striving for self-sufficiency – is not only reactionary but also not viable in economic terms. This version of 'economic sovereignty' is thus not a realistic option. Yet to present the socialist economies as a way out, after their collapse in Eastern Europe, would not be particularly fruitful. Notions of sovereignty and national independence for that matter have a mixed legacy. We need not call for a return to De Valera's economic strategy just because we recognize the need for national economic development, which is a worthwhile and progressive aim in terms of people's needs. Nor is the seeking of economic sovereignty necessarily a reactionary and chauvinist pipe-dream, if we redefine it in terms of achieving democratic control over economic affairs and a refusal to accept an outward-oriented and exploitative model of dependent development. Non-dependent development may be a difficult (perhaps impossible) objective to achieve, but it must be part of an alternative economic strategy in Ireland.

The overriding objective of a democratic economic strategy should be to meet the main social and economic aspirations of the Irish people. This alternative strategy would have to redress the balance of economic power to alleviate poverty, reduce unemployment dramatically and end the necessity felt by the young to emigrate. As the *Democratic Programme* adopted by the First Dáil of 1919 put it, this strategy would seek 'To promote the development of [Ireland's] resources . . . in the interest and to the benefit of the Irish people.'[18] To obtain the resources to do so, one can either redistribute existing resources in a more equitable manner or, what is arguably more sustainable, create new resources by a growth in the national income. A policy of macro-economic populism (simple redistribution) has been shown to be both economically and politically unviable. Nor is the orthodox economic focus on growth rates without considering redistribution any more viable. What we can consider, as a broad strategic aim, is growth through redistribution. This would not only create the resources to meet the social needs outlined above but would also be economically beneficial insofar as it could create higher, demand-led rates of growth.

It may seem somewhat of a cliché to state that production should be based on social need rather than profit, but it is nevertheless the basis of a democratic economy. It may also be difficult to achieve a community of free and equal citizens deciding consciously upon the general framework of economic and social life, but it remains a worthwhile objective. Nothing that has happened in Eastern Europe negates these general ideas, although of course the collapse of what has passed as socialism for a whole era, makes its achievement much more difficult. What an alternative economic strategy seeks to do is bridge the gap between the present economic crisis and that vision of a possible future. It is no use producing a rosy vision of an Éire Nua, if no viable path for its attainment is outlined. An economic programme must respond to people's basic concern with job security, land tenure, the cost of living, availability of housing, education for their children and so on. Without this type of programme, calls for national liberation and democratic socialism will be viewed with justifiable scepticism by many. The Workers' Party has stated that 'we offer a plan that *even under the present system* will immediately protect the Irish working class from the misery of the current crisis of capitalism in Ireland'.[19] Unfortunately such a plan does not exist – if it did the government would have adopted it by now. Nor can that plan be realistic if it ignores the partition of Ireland. Nevertheless, it points towards the need for short- and medium-term objectives to bridge the gap between the economic system we have at present and the democratic economy we might aspire to.

Economic planning has had a bad press since the collapse of the state socialist economies in Eastern Europe and the apparent reasserted sovereignty of the market elsewhere. Yet in the above section considering what more of the same might mean for the Irish economy, we found little to hope for from a free-market perspective. A democratic independent Irish economy would need to control key economic sectors, including high technology, which would allow it to effect planning agreements with the private sector. A democratic economic strategy would need to exercise more control than exists at present over foreign investment. The struggle against dependent development does not, however, entail a knee-jerk reaction against multinational companies. A national democratic strategy would seek to match the requirements of investors with the country's development plan, stressing those projects which were a social priority or had a strong export potential for example. In this way the uneven development of the Irish economy caused by partition and the consolidation of monopoly capitalism could be gradually undone. This could be achieved neither by a return to a mythical era of decent national capitalism, nor by a Cambodian-type move towards a primitive autarky.

Much of the discussion on how market and plan can be combined to form a democratic socialist market model has been confused. State socialism and rigid centralized planning has clearly led to bureaucracy, economic dislocation and, ultimately, a crippling inefficiency. Yet, for the Irish economy it is easy to envisage the advantages of democratic national control over natural resources, the major economic units and the banks, to allow for the national coordination of economic activity. A market though – that is, goods being allocated through supply and demand – can help avoid some of the problems involved in allocating and co-ordinating without a popular mandate or democratic participation. The challenge would be to find the mechanisms for people to contribute to a national economic strategy at a realistic (local, perhaps county) level. If we move away from the vocabulary of nationalization, with its image of inefficient centrally administered state corporations, and speak of 'socialization' or 'social ownership' this debate would be clearer. Social ownership may take various forms, depending on the circumstances: state corporations certainly, but also cooperatives, self-managed enterprises, and even undertakings combining private and public elements. The point is that there should not be, indeed cannot be, a rigid blueprint for a democratic economy.

Some radical economists argue that the capitalist world economy is now so integrated across national boundaries that an autonomous national economic strategy is simply no longer possible. Certainly this reality makes impossible any naive vision of economic self-sufficiency in Ireland. Yet a national strategy for development is both necessary and possible. It is at the national level that demands for social changes are articulated and it is control of the national state which provides the essential platform for social transformation. This does not mean that we advocate a reactionary, inward-looking Ireland where the 'comely maidens' and 'athletic youths' De Valera referred to can live in isolation. On the contrary, the alternative economic strategy advocated must have an international dimension. International capital should not be opposed by national chauvinism (rarely successful anyway) but by internationalization of the alternative economic strategy and democratic decision making of each country. In the meantime, democratic opposition movements (especially but not exclusively in Europe) can seek what unites them rather than simply bemoaning the power of transnational capital and a mythical 'Brussels'.

An alternative democratic economic strategy will not materialize without a considerable increase in popular participation. At the moment the economy, or at least economic policymaking, seems remote from most peoples's lives. A democratic economic policy will only emerge in the context of a peace settlement leading to the creation of a national democracy in Ireland. If and when that occurs people's participation will increase in all spheres, including the economy. In the meantime, we can see examples of sporadic attempts by people to enforce democratic accountability over the economy. The siting of a toxic waste disposal plant will create local resistance. The closure of a transnational plant will lead to protest, even factory occupations. As the economic crises recur and become deeper (a likely prospect as we have seen above) so there will be more and more localized (and perhaps national) attempts to counteract it. Trade unions, cooperatives, women's groups and community groups will all take action. It is through these actions and campaigns that a genuinely democratic economic alternative might take shape.

Geoff Hodgson, in a book on *The Democratic Economy*, has argued that: 'Socialism is not simply planning for social need; it is planning within a system in which the determination of those needs can be criticised or scrutinised from alternative viewpoints.'[20] In other words, socialism is simply not possible without the widest democracy at all levels of society. For example, concerns about the environment should be a central part of the economic decision-making process. The need for equality between the sexes will likewise be a central element in the economic process. Conflict will not disappear in a democratic society and a national economic plan will not reconcile all interests in society. The point is that pluralistic democracy is as essential to the economic process as it is to a healthy political system. It is no coincidence that in 1981 the Polish trade-union Solidarity demanded in the same breath 'political pluralism of opinions and transformation of the economy and the state according to the spirit of democracy'. A national democracy in Ireland will also be impossible until both these elements are achieved. What is certain is that they are inseparable.

Some trade unions are already calling for a 'popular planning' alternative to the present economic system. This is a type of planning which begins from people's concerns and not the need to sustain private profit. It entails popular participation in and democratic control over economic planning, as against the so-called National Economic Plans that governments regularly provide, usually to unburden the cost of the economic crisis on to ordinary people. This trade union economic alternative 'demands not only more resources, re-organisation of the development effort, more popular participation and public account-ability, but also a conceptual rethinking of economic priorities'.[21] The last point could be related to the ever more pressing concern with the environment. The only criticism of this call for a democratic economy is that it is directed solely to six-county trade unionists and not to the people of Ireland as a whole. Extended in that way, and made more 'grounded' by involving many other interest groups, this type of strategy could yet bear fruit.

We have now concluded our panoramic overview of the main alternative scenarios open to the Irish economy. Continuation of present trends, while not leading to some mythical 'collapse of capitalism', will almost certainly not meet people's needs in either Irish state. An evolutionary and cooperative re-unification on its own is simply not enough and some kind of democratic transformation of the economy would need to occur. The presently underused and misused resources of the Irish economy, North and South could be unlocked. A more interventionist industrial policy based on this potential unleashing of energy would certainly be possible. A more equitable distribution of resources would equally provide a dynamic impetus to the economy. To strive for a non-dependent model of development based on popular planning and accountability would not be 'pie in the sky' if linked to an alternative economic strategy based on a viable, credible and popular democratic economy. In this way, the mode of regulation of the Irish economy, which we have traced in earlier chapters through its various forms, would gradually become a *social* regulation of the production process, as opposed to a market regulation wholly based on the *individual* pursuit of profit.

Conclusions

One way to finish is to return to the beginning. Chapter 1 began by setting out the main planks of the 'dependent development' approach. This has been referred to at various points in the subsequent chapters. Now we need to ask the very simple, yet important, question: 1. Is Ireland a dependent economy? Then we must try to answer its sequel: 2. If so, is a *non*-dependent development possible? Our own democratic alternative economic strategy does indeed assume that this option exists. The role of the multinational corporations, the state and economic planning all hinge around these two questions. We shall try to avoid simplistic, premature or dogmatic answers to our questions.

As to the overall record of the 26 counties, Joe Lee has no doubts, calling it the 'least impressive' in Europe this century and asking ironically, 'How has Ireland achieved and sustained this level of relative retardation?'[22] Yet even this low ranking in the European economic league table hides the full picture. Living standards which at least approximate to the levels of the advanced industrial societies have been achieved at the cost of high emigration and population decline. As O'Malley points out this has 'allowed the average incomes of the remaining population to be fairly high despite economic weakness'.[23] Foreign borrowing and EC subsidies further helped to create this image of relative prosperity.

There is thus a prima-facie case that Irish development has not been successful. Is it, however, a dependent economy, some 70 years after the 26 counties broke from Britain? Recalling our introductory chapter, foreign domination over the key economic sectors was a major sign of dependence. Eoin O'Malley has demonstrated conclusively the absolutely dominant role of the transnational corporations in the Southern economy: by the 1980s they accounted for one-third of employment but a full three-quarters of manufactured exports.[24] The drain on the economic surplus produced can be gauged from the fact that in 1990 the outflow of profits, dividends and royalties from the Republic was £2.34m which represented 10 per cent of the GDP. Clearly if these profits are not being reinvested in Ireland they represent a net loss to the country's future growth potential. If in the nineteenth century the main form of dependency was unequal exchange, today it is mediated through not only the transnational corporations but also the foreign debt. As noted in Chapter 2 the foreign debt of the Republic has now reached over £24b which represents over 100 per cent of GNP. These loans are part of the modern form of imperialism and countries like Ireland are mortgaging their independence (and part of their income to pay the interest) by pursuing this type of dependent development.

As to the 'internal' aspects of development, apart from persisting poverty, unemployment and emigration, we can point to the failure of the indigenous bourgeoisie to implement national development. Here again Joe Lee provides a scathing critique:

> Sixty years after independence, fifty years after blanket protection, twenty years after the Committee on Industrial Organisation, fifteen years after the Anglo-Irish Free Trade Agreement, eight years after entering the EEC, a native entrepreneurial cadre of the requisite quality had failed to emerge.[25]

It could not even compete effectively on the home market, let alone the world market. By the mid 1980s, the net output per person engaged in foreign-owned industries was £42,500 whereas the equivalent output in indigenous firms was a mere £17,000. Certainly this was not due to some psychological inadequacy of the native entrepreneur but it does reflect one of the key structural characteristics of the dependency situation. What it leads to, again typical of the dependency situation, is not only an increased role for the state in creating the conditions for industrialization but also as an active player in that regard. In the North of Ireland the weakness of indigenous industry and the role of the state in sustaining development is even more pronounced.

We should not, of course pretend that Ireland is in the same situation as Haiti, for example, as some simplistic attempts to 'apply' dependency theory have hinted. On the other hand, we cannot neglect the depth of the crisis facing the dependent development model in Ireland. Raymond Crotty, for example, writes that 'Irish agriculture is in its worst crisis since the 1840s. Now, as then, agriculture's crisis will reverberate throughout the economy, causing new insolvencies, job losses, increased unemployment and increased emigration.'[26] If agriculture faces a serious crisis the failings of industrial policy in the South are just as evident. The government sponsored Telesis Report of 1982 had already at that time pointed to the deeprooted structural problems caused by dependence on foreign investment. Telesis noted how foreign-owned industry operated as an enclave with few linkages with the rest of the economy. Moreover, Telesis argued, correctly, that no sustained economic development was possible without a dynamic indigenous industrial base. This diagnosis was repeated in the 1992 Culliton Report but, again, decisive action seems unlikely. Agriculture, especially given its current crisis, has proven unable to act as a springboard for industrialization either, as might have been expected. Producing a favourable 'climate' for private enterprise, as the current wisdom advises, seems unlikely to overcome the structural/historical fruits of dependency.

If the Republic is facing a development crossroads, Northern Ireland is facing a development crisis. Here dependency on Britain takes on an obvious and overbearing role due to the continued political link. Not even the pretence of self-sustained growth is possible. Underlying weaknesses have only been masked by continued British government intervention to prop up the North's economy. The Northern Ireland Economic Council in a farreaching discussion of economic policy admits freely that 'in terms of the principal indicators of economic well-being Northern Ireland has lagged well behind most if not all other regions [in the UK], and many of our chronic economic and industrial problems remain largely unresolved'.[27] The private sector can simply not survive without substantial and continuing government aid. The foreign-owned sector (including British investment) has declined dramatically in importance, employing 87,500 people in 1973 and 41,000 in 1990. As in the South, current economic wisdom (as expressed in the British government's 'Competing in the 1990s') advocates a reduction of state intervention, with the government simply assisting in creating the right 'climate' for an ill-defined 'competitiveness', where market forces rule supreme.

If we accept that Ireland in broad terms follows the pattern of dependent economies we will need to ask whether a *non*-dependent development alternative exists. We cannot, in all honesty, point to Cuba as a successful socialist model of development applicable to the island of Ireland. We also need to confront the argument that Ireland simply has no alternative as a small open economy but to be export-oriented and practise social austerity programmes to survive in the world economy.

In the case of Ireland today a non-dependent development could be summarized, according to Bob Rowthorn under two main headings:

1. Diversity

A country which sells most of its exports to a single country or small group of countries is highly vulnerable to adverse political or economic events in those countries. It is open to economic blackmail and may also suffer grievously if some of these countries undergo a severe recession. Likewise, a country which depends heavily on the export of just a few products will be highly vulnerable to fluctuations in world market conditions. This is the basic weakness of economies based on monoculture (for example, sugar or coffee in Latin America). To reduce this kind of vulnerability it is desirable for a country to export a fairly wide variety of different products to a wide variety of different countries. Just how wide depends on the circumstances, but ideally the range should be wide enough to guard against major fluctuations. Similar considerations apply in the case of imports. Of course, no country can insulate itself entirely against external shocks, but insulation against shocks is an important dimension of economic autonomy. Over the past 30 years Ireland has diversified its import and export structure considerably, both with regard to product variety and trading partners. In this respect, the economy is arguably much less 'dependent' than it used to be. Certainly, it is much less dependent on economic conditions in Britain than was the case 30 years ago. The recent financial crisis in the Republic following Britain's withdrawl from the ERM might qualify this statement.

2. Flexibility and creativity

Successful development requires not just insulation against external shocks, but also both the ability to respond to long-term adverse shifts in the world economy and the ability to seize new opportunities as they arise. Such abilities have both cultural and institutional dimensions. For example, the workforce must have, or be in a position to acquire fairly easily, the skills required for new kinds of production. Firms must possess the managerial skills to move into new areas, and the willingness and freedom to do so. Economic policy and the state apparatus must facilitate the required redirection of economic activity. These are not easy problems to solve and particular difficulties arise in the Irish context because of the strong presence of foreign-owned firms, which may have little desire to move into new areas of production or into higher value-added activities which offer better long-term prospects for the Irish population (R&D, design marketing etc). Many of them may see Ireland as merely a low-wage base for simpler forms of processing, assembly and the like, whilst preferring other countries for their more sophisticated and knowledge-intensive operations.[28]

So in terms of diversification the Republic can be seen to have moved beyond the 'neo-colonial' relationship with Britain, but flexibility and creativity (not to mention sustainable dynamic growth) are still thwarted by the dependence on foreign investment. An alternative economic strategy has indeed been argued by various government advisory bodies. For the South, the Telesis Report of 1982 is still an important benchmark. It recommended that the state should take a broader and more long-term view of development than at present, with strategic state initiatives in key sectors. The state should also insist that foreign investors locate research and development activities in the country and promote linkages with the local economy. More recently, the National and Economic Social Council has called for long-term policies directed towards resolving structural problems in industry and agriculture, and, most ambitiously, 'the removal of major inequities in society'.[29] Trade-union involvement in this type of economic planning with a social dimension seems likely to continue in the South, although this dimension tends to fade when economic conditions worsen.

For the North, the Northern Ireland Economic Council (NIEC) has severely criticized recent British government proposals on the economy for relying too heavily on market mechanisms. It argues that only the state is in a position to break the region out of its 'vicious circle of decline because of its peripherality [and], outmoded industrial structure'.[30] The NIEC for its part advocates a 'broad focus strategy', not unlike that of the NESC in the South, which it explicitly compares to the 'indicative planning' practised in France in the 1960s. Yet these alternative strategies have very definite political limits because they assume a continuation of the present constitutional status quo and, of course, private-property relations. Furthermore, these economic institutions tend, as Lee notes, 'to seek instant solutions to immediate problems. The premium is on tunnel thinking, blind to either long-term perspective or lateral linkage'.[31] One major underlying problem is the continual stress laid on excluding 'non-economic' issues from economic debate.

There is thus the makings of a viable alternative economic strategy already being mooted which we could call, by no means pejoratively, reformist. Our own proposed democratic economic plan is more radical in various respects. With regard to transnational corporations we recognize (against some radical writers) their positive, albeit contradictory, development role. A radical democratic economic strategy, while stressing the centrality of indigenous development, would continue to attract foreign investment. The difference is that it would seek to operate within the logic of a national economic development plan. On Europe our attitude also goes against the grain of most radical writers, considering that withdrawal from the EC is not realistic. Instead we propose European-level alternative economic strategies which, amongst other things, could more effectively control the transnational corporations. It is on the question of partition where the truly radical implications of our national democratic strategy become more evident. Operating with a completely different logic from that of the British Labour Party and Fianna Fail's 'technocratic anti-partitionism'[32] this type of unification would unlock much of the thwarted potential of the 'hidden Ireland'. It is therefore, not a romantic nostalgia for a closed national economy which we advocate but a realistic, radical and internationalist strategy for the 1990s.

No one today would advocate a literal return to De Valera's economics of self-sufficiency because, quite simply, they would not be viable. Yet the *principles* enunciated by Keynes at his 1933 lecture in Dublin (see p.28) retain their relevance. There he spoke positively about economic nationalism against the prevalent liberal free-trade orthodoxy. Though aware of the limits of self-sufficiency in a small country, he welcomed its strengthening in Ireland. Joe Lee has more recently taken up this theme in a broad retrospective survey where he concludes that: 'There is little point bewailing factors beyond one's control until one has taken steps necessary to achieve the best results from those within one's control. That is the enduring validity of the original Sinn Fein thought.'[33] Though obviously vulnerable to international forces beyond our control a united democratic Ireland *could* devise a strategy of national economic development based on growth through redistribution. Self-sustaining and dynamic growth will by no means be easy to achieve. Our analysis shows, however, that dependency reversal – in its external but also internal aspects – is a prerequisite for a democratic future. What we must stress, on a final note, is that in economic strategy, be it in mainstream or alternative debates, politics is always in command.

Notes

Chapter 1: Dependent Development

1. R. Crotty, *Ireland in Crisis*, Dingle, Brandon, 1986, p. 23.
2. L.M. Cullen, *An Economic History of Ireland since 1660*, London, Batsford, 1972, p. 9.
3. Ibid, p. 37.
4. Crotty, *Ireland in Crisis*, p. 207.
5. E. O'Malley, *Industry and Economic Development*, Dublin, Gill and Macmillan, 1989, p. 37.
6. Cullen, *An Economic History*, p. 93.
7. L. Kennedy, 'The rural economy, 1820–1914', in L. Kennedy and P. Ollerenshaw (eds) *An Economic History of Ulster*, Manchester, Manchester University Press, 1985, p. 13.
8. Ibid, p. 15.
9. Crotty, *Ireland in Crisis*, p. 42.
10. K. Kennedy, T. Giblin and D, McHugh, *The Economic Development of Ireland in the Twentieth Century*, London, Routledge, 1988, p. 12.
11. Sinn Fein, 16.12.1911.
12. Cullen, *An Economic History*, p. 96.
13. Crotty, *Ireland in Crisis*, p. 47.
14. E.R. Green, 'Industrial decline in the nineteenth century', in L. Cullen (ed.) *The Formation of the Irish Economy*, Cork, Mercier Press, 1979, p. 92.
15. Cullen, *An Economic History*, p. 132.
16. K. Marx and F. Engels, *Ireland and the Irish Question*, Moscow, Progress, 1971, p. 106.
17. Cullen, *An Economic History*, p. 150.
18. Ibid, p. 146.
19. O'Malley, *Industry and Economic Development*, p. 49.
20. M. Hechter, *Internal Colonialism*, London, Routledge, 1975, p. 92.
21. Marx and Engels, *Ireland*, p. 148.
22. Ibid, p. 132.
23. O'Malley, *Industry and Economic Development*, p. 51.

24. B. Girvin, *Between Two Worlds: Politics and Economy in Independent Ireland*, Dublin, Gill and Macmillan, 1989, p. 7.
25. O'Malley, *Industry and Economic Development*, p. 52.
26. Cullen, *An Economic History*, p. 167.
27. Ibid, p. 159.
28. Ibid, p. 160.
29. Ibid, p. 172.
30. Ibid, p. 164.
31. P. Gibbon, *The Origins of Ulster Unionism*, Manchester, Manchester University Press, 1975, p. 137.
32. M. Daly, *A Social and Economic History of Ireland since 1800*, Dublin, The Educational Company, 1980, p. 79.
33. Ibid, p. 88.
34. Ibid, p. 71.
35. B. Girvin, *Between Two Worlds*.

Chapter 2: The Southern Economy

1. J. Mokyr, *Why Ireland Starved: A Quantitative and Analytical History of the Irish Economy, 1800–1850*, London, Allen and Unwin, 1985, p. 279.
2. P. Bairoch, 'The main trends in national economic disparities since the industrial revolution', in P. Bairoch and M. Levy-Lebazer (eds), *Disparities in Economic Development since the Industrial Revolution*, New York, St Martin's Press, 1981, Table 1.6.
3. K. Kennedy, T. Giblin and D, McHugh, *The Economic Development of Ireland in the Twentieth Century*, London, Routledge, 1988, p. 21.
4. M. Hechter, *Internal Colonialism: The Celtic Fringe in British National Development, 1536–1966*, London, Routledge, 1975, p. 92.
5. Mokyr, *Why Ireland Starved*, p. 289.
6. D. Johnson, *The Inter-war Economy in Ireland*, Dublin, Economic and Social History Society, 1985, p. 5.
7. L.M. Cullen, *An Economic History of Ireland since 1660*, London, Batsford, 1981, p. 171–2.
8. Kennedy et al., *The Economic Development of Ireland*, p. 75.
9. Cited in ibid, p. 35.
10. F.S.L. Lyons, *Ireland since the Famine*, London, Fontana, 1981, p. 614.
11. Kennedy et al., *The Economic Development of Ireland*, p. 52.
12. A. Gramsci, *Selections from the Prison Notebooks*, London, Lawrence and Wishart, 1971, p. 109.
13. F.S. Lyons, 'De Valera revisited', *Magill*, March 1981, p. 61.
14. T.K. Whitaker, 'From protection to free trade – the Irish case', *Administration*, Winter 1973, p. 415.

15. Department of Finance, *Economic Development*, Dublin, Stationery Office, 1958, p. 2.
16. R. Crotty, *Ireland in Crisis*, Dingle, Brandon, 1986, p. 92.
17. M. McDowell, 'A generation of public expenditure growth: Leviathan unchained', in F. Litton (ed.) *Unequal Achievement: The Irish Experience 1957–1982*, Dublin, Institute of Public Administration, 1982, p. 184.
18. Kennedy et al., *The Economic Development of Ireland*, p. 72.
19. Crotty, *Ireland in Crisis*, p. 11.
20. Kennedy et al., *The Economic Development of Ireland*, p. 77.
21. Crotty, *Ireland in Crisis*, p. 7.
22. P. Bew, E. Hazelkorn and H. Patterson, *The Dynamics of Irish Politics*, London, Lawrence and Wishart, 1988, p. 129.
23. Ibid, p. 123.
24. E. O'Malley, 'Dependency and the experience of industry in the Republic of Ireland', IDS Bulletin, 12, 1, 1980, p. 45.
25. R. Stanton, 'Foreign investment and host country politics: the Irish case' in D. Seers, B. Schaffer and M.L. Kiljunen (eds) *Under-developed Europe: Studies in Core–Periphery Relations*, Brighton, Harvester, 1979, p. 120.
26. The Economist Intelligence Unit, *Ireland to 1992: Putting Its House in Order?*, London, EIU, 1988, p. 73.
27. H. O'Neill, *Spatial Planning in the Small Economy: A Case Study of Ireland*, New York, Praeger, 1971, p. 5.
28. L. Gibbons, 'Coming out of hibernation? The myth of modernity in Irish culture', in R. Kearney (ed.) *Across the Frontiers: Ireland in the 1990s*, Dublin, Wolfhound Press, 1988, p. 218.
29. The Economist Intelligence Unit, *Ireland to 1992*, p. 2.
30. Ibid.
31. Crotty, *Ireland in Crisis*, p. 80.
32. The Economist Intelligence Unit, *Ireland to 1992*, p. 7.

Chapter 3: The Northern Economy

1. J. Othick, 'The economic history of Ulster: a perspective', in L. Kennedy and P. Ollerenshaw (eds) *An Economic History of Ulster, 1820–1940*, Manchester, Manchester University Press, 1985, p. 238.
2. J. Goldstrom, 'The industrialisation of the north-east', in L.M. Cullen (ed.) *The Formation of the Irish Economy*, Cork, Mercier Press, 1976, p. 107.
3. Ibid, p. 108.
4. Othick, 'The economic history of Ulster', p. 232.
5. Ibid, p. 229.
6. K. Kennedy, T. Giblin and D. McHugh, *The Economic Development of Ireland in the Twentieth Century*, London, Routledge, 1988, p. 95.

7. D. Senghaas, *The European Experience*, Leamington Spa, Berg Publishers, 1985, p. 120.
8. F.S. Lyons, *Ireland since the Famine*, London, Fontana, 1981 p. 289.
9. See for example, M.H. Watkins, 'A staple theory of economic growth', in W.T. Easterbrook and M.H. Watkins (eds) *Approaches to Canadian Economic History*, Toronto, 1967.
10. T. Wilson, *Ulster: Conflict and Consent*, Oxford, Basil Blackwell, 1989, p. 77.
11. Cited by P. Bew, P. Gibbon and H. Patterson, *The State in Northern Ireland 1921–72*, Manchester, Manchester University Press, 1979, p. 53.
12. Kennedy et al., *The Economic Development of Ireland*, p. 108.
13. P. Buckland, *A History of Northern Ireland*, Dublin, Gill and Macmillan, 1981, p. 74.
14. Ibid, p. 83.
15. Wilson, *Ulster*, p. 85.
16. Bew et al., *The State in Northern Ireland*, p. 54.
17. L. O'Dowd, 'Trends and potential of the service sector in Northern Ireland', in P. Teague (ed.) *Beyond the Rhetoric: Politics, the Economy and Social Policy in Northern Ireland*, London, Lawrence and Wishart, 1987, p. 190.
18. Wilson, *Ulster*, p. 96.
19. B. Rowthorn and N. Wayne, *Northern Ireland: The Political Economy of Conflict*, Oxford, Polity Press, 1988, p. 74.
20. J. Bradley, V.N. Hewitt and C.W. Jefferson, *Industrial Location Policy and Equality of Opportunity in Assisted Employment in Northern Ireland 1949–1981*, Belfast, FEA, 1986, p. 21.
21. Wilson, *Ulster*, p. 91.
22. Bew et al., *The State in Northern Ireland*, p. 153.
23. Ibid, p. 190.
24. Rowthorn and Wayne, *Northern Ireland*, p. 94.
25. D. Canning, B. Moore and J. Rhodes, 'Economic growth in Northern Ireland: problems and prospects', in Teague (ed.) *Beyond the Rhetoric*, p. 211.
26. P. Teague, 'Multinational companies in the Northern Ireland economy: an outmoded model of industrial development?', in Teague (ed.) *Beyond the Rhetoric*, p. 169.
27. D. Hamilton, 'Industrial development policy in Northern Ireland – an evaluation of the IDB', *Economic and Social Review*, 22, 1, 1990, p. 65.
28. L. O'Dowd, B. Rolston and M. Tomlinson, 'From Labour to the Tories: the ideology of containment in Northern Ireland', *Capital and Class*, 18, 1982, p. 88.
29. Rowthorn and Wayne, *Northern Ireland*, p. 98.
30. NIEC, *Economic Strategy: Overall Review*, Report 73, March 1989, p. 15.
31. NIEC, *Economic Assessment*, p. 66.

32. Ibid, p. 48.
33. Ibid, p. 47.
34. B. Rolston and M. Tomlinson, *Unemployment in West Belfast: The Obair Report*, Belfast, Beyond the Pale Publications, 1988, p. 132.
35. NIEC, *The Industrial Development Board for Northern Ireland*, Report 79, February 1990, p. 81.
36. Canning et al., 'Economic growth in Northern Ireland', p. 227.
37. Cited in Kennedy et al., *The Economic Development of Ireland*, p. 116.

Chapter 4: Workers and the Economy

1. D. Rothman and P. O'Connell, 'The changing social structure of Ireland', in F. Litton (ed.) *Unequal Achievement: The Irish Experience 1957–1982*, Dublin, Institute of Public Administration, 1982, p. 72.
2. R. Breen, D. Hannan, D. Rottman and C. Whelan, *Understanding Contemporary Ireland*, Basingstoke, Macmillan, 1990, p. 86.
3. Ibid, p. 87.
4. T. Callan, B. Nolan, C. Whelan and D. Hannan, *Poverty, Welfare and Income in Ireland*, Dublin, ESRI, 1989.
5. F. Gafikin and M. Morrissey, 'Poverty and politics in Northern Ireland', in P. Teague (ed.) *Beyond the Rhetoric: Politics, the Economy and Social Policy in Northern Ireland*, London, Lawrence and Wishart, 1987, p. 144.
6. The Economist Intelligence Unit, *Ireland to 1992*, Special Report No 1137, London, EIU, 1988, p. 93.
7. K. Kennedy, T. Giblin and D. McHugh, *The Economic Development of Ireland in the Twentieth Century*, London, Routledge, 1988, p. 262.
8. Ibid, p. 145.
9. Breen et al., *Understanding Contemporary Ireland*, p. 146.
10. Callan et al., *Poverty, Welfare and Income in Ireland*, p. 180.
11. NIEC, *Economic Strategy: Overall Review*, Report 73, Belfast, March 1989, p. 8.
12. B. Rolston and M. Tomlinson, *Unemployment in West Belfast: The Obair Report*, Belfast, Beyond the Pale Publications, 1988, p. 71.
13. Ibid, p. 134.
14. D. Fitzpatrick, *Irish Emigration 1801–1921*, Dublin, The Economic and Social History Society of Ireland, 1984, p. 38.
15. Cited in Kennedy et al., *The Economic Development of Ireland*, p. 15.
16. Ibid.
17. Economist Intelligence Unit, *Ireland to 1992*, p. 18.
18. Ibid, p. 93.

19. NIEC, *Demographic Trends in Northern Ireland*, Report 57, Belfast, April 1986, p. 85.
20. Ibid, p. 46.
21. Cited in Breen et al., *Understanding of Contemporary Ireland*, p. 117.
22. J. Blackwell, 'Government, economy and society', in F. Litton (ed.) *Unequal Achievement*, p. 49.
23. J. Trewsdale, *The Aftermath of Recession: Changing Patterns in Female Employment in Northern Ireland*, Belfast, Equal Opportunities Commission, 1987, Woman Power No 4, p. 38.
24. Ibid, p. 46.
25. Fair Employment Agency, *An Industrial and Occupational Profile of the Two Sections of the Population in Northern Ireland*, Belfast, FEA, 1987, p. 14.
26. R. Osborne and R. Cormack, *Religion, Occupations and Employment, 1971–81*, Belfast, FEA, 1987, Research Paper No 11, p. 101.
27. *Fair Employment in Northern Ireland*, London, HMSO, 1988, p. 47.
28. P. Compton, 'Demographic and geographical aspects of the unemployment differential between Protestants and Roman Catholics in Northern Ireland', in P. Compton (ed.) *The Contemporary Population of Northern Ireland and Population-related Issues*, Belfast, Queen's University, 1981.
29. Cited in V. McCormack and J. O'Hara, *Enduring Inequality: Religious Discrimination in Employment in Northern Ireland*, London, National Council for Civil Liberties, 1990, p. 14.
30. Rev. W. McCrea, MP Cited in Rolston and Tomlinson, *Unemployment in West Belfast*, p. 56.
31. Ibid.
32. T. Wilson, *Ulster: Conflict and Consent*, London, Basil Blackwell, 1989, p. 108.
33. Ibid, p. 116.
34. B. Rowthorn and N. Wayne, *Northern Ireland: The Political Economy of Conflict*, London, Polity Press, 1988, p. 34.

Chapter 6: Europe and 1992

1. A. Coughlan, 'Ireland' in D. Seers and C. Vaistsos (eds) *Integration and Unequal Development: The Experience of the EEC*, London, Macmillan, 1980, p. 124.
2. P. Hainsworth, 'Northern Ireland in the European Community', in M. Keating and B. Jones (eds) *Regions in the European Community*, Oxford, Clarendon Press, 1985, p. 109.
3. S. Dooney, 'The economics of 1992', *European Economy*, 35, 1988, pp. 151–2.

4. Coughlan, 'Ireland', p. 127.
5. Dooney, 'The economics of 1992', p. 153.
6. Economist Intelligence Unit, *Ireland to 1992: Putting its House in Order*, London, EIU, 1988, p. 67.
7. Ibid, p.69.
8. Commission of the European Communities, *The Regions of the Enlarged Community: Third Periodic Report on the Social and Economic Situation and Development of the Regions of the Community*, Luxembourg, EC, 1987, p. 1181.
9. Coughlan, 'Ireland', p. 130.
10. Hainsworth, 'Northern Ireland', p. 118.
11. Ibid, p. 118.
12. Ibid, p. 123.
13. *Northern Ireland Regional Development Plan*, HMSO, 1989, p. 14.
14. P. Teague, 'Multinational companies in the Northern Ireland economy: an outmoded model of industrial development', in P. Teague (ed.) *Beyond the Rhetoric: Politics, the Economy and Social Policy in Northern Ireland*, London, Lawrence and Wishart, 1987, p. 177.
15. Labour Research Department, *1992: What it Means to Trade Unionists*, London, LRD, 1989, p. 3.
16. Ibid, p.4.
17. P. Cecchini, *The European Challenge – 1992 – The Benefits of a Single Market*, London, Wildwood House, 1988, p. xix.
18. Ibid, p. xx.
19. Ibid, p. xi.
20. Labour Research Department, '1992', p. 15.
21. SDLP, *1992: The Implications of the Single Market for Northern Ireland*, Belfast, Social Democratic and Labour Party, 1988, p. 3.
22. Bloxham Maguire, *Irish Economic and Financial Outlook – with a Special Summary of our Analysis on Ireland and the EEC Internal Market in 1992*, Dublin, 1988, p. 3.
23. Economist Intelligence Unit, *Ireland to 1992*, p. 108.
24. Ibid, p. 114.
25. SDLP, *1992*, pp. 3–4.
26. Ibid, p. 2.
27. *Northern Ireland Regional Development Plan*, p. 15.
28. Economist Intelligence Unit, *Ireland to 1992*, p. 115.
29. H. Morrissey, *Women in Ireland: The Impact of 1992*, Belfast, Amalgamated Transport and General Workers Union, 1989, p. 9.
30. Ibid, p. 104.
31. Cecchini, *The European Challenge*, p. 104.
32. Economist Intelligence Unit, *Ireland to 1992*, p.74.

33. J.O Siochru, *An Introduction to 1992 and its Implications for Trade Unions*, Dublin, SUS Research Ltd, 1988, p. 7.
34. J. Grahl and P. Teague, *1992: The Big Market*, London, Lawrence and Wishart, 1990, p. 327.

Chapter 7: Alternative Scenarios

1. J.J. Lee, *Ireland 1912–85: Politics and Society*, Cambridge, Cambridge University Press, 1989.
2. R. Rowthorn, 'Northern Ireland: an Economy in Crisis', in P. Teague (ed.) *Beyond the Rhetoric*, London, Lawrence and Wishart, 1987.
3. R. Crotty, *Ireland in Crisis: A Study in Capitalist Colonial Undevelopment*, Dingle, Brandon, 1986.
4. S. Roper and G. Gudgin, *Economic Forecasts for Northern Ireland, 1991–2000*, Northern Ireland Economic Research Centre, Belfast, March 1991.
5. The Economic and Social Research Institute, *Quarterly Economic Commentary*, Dublin, December 1990.
6. National and Economic Social Council, *Ireland in the European Community: Performance, Prospects and Strategy*, 88, Dublin, August 1989.
7. Northern Ireland Economic Council, *The Industrial Development Board for Northern Ireland: Selective Financial Assistance and Economic Development Policy*, Report No 79, Belfast, February 1990.
8. G. Gudgin M. Hart, J. Fagg, E. D'arcy and R. Keegan, *Job Generation in Manufacturing Industry 1973–86: a Comparison of Northern Ireland with the Republic of Ireland and the English Midlands*, Belfast, Northern Ireland Economic Research Centre, June 1989.
9. See Hitchens, Wagner and Birnie (*Closing the Productivity Gap*, Aldershot, Avebury, 1990) for an analysis of relative productivity in Northern Ireland, the results, methodology and policy recommendations of which have been the subject of some debate and criticism,
10. Northern Ireland Economic Council, *Economic Assessment: April 1990*. Report No 81, Belfast, 1990.
11. P. McGregor and V. Borooah, 'Poverty and the distribution of income in Northern Ireland', *Economic and Social Review*, 22, 2, January 1991.
12. Department of Industry and Commerce, *Review of Industrial Performance 1990*, Dublin, The Stationery Office, 1990.
13. L. de Paor, *Unfinished Business: Ireland Today and Tomorrow*, London, Hutchinson Radius, 1990.
14. See for example Wilson's introduction to *The Northern Ireland Economy: a Comparative Study in the Economic Development of a Peripheral Region*, R. Harris, C. Jefferson and J. Spencer (eds), London, Longman, 1990.

15. A practice adopted by transnational companies (TNC's) which through intra-firm trading exploits low tax countries and enables TNC's to maximize profits.

16. E. O'Malley, *Industry and Economic Development: the Challenge for the Latecomer*, Dublin, Gill and Macmillan, 1989.

17. K. Allen, *Is Southern Ireland a Neo-Colony?*, Dublin, Bookmarks, 1990, p. 43.

18. See M. Comerford, *The First Dáil*, Dublin, 1971.

19. Sinn Fein/The Workers' Party, *The Irish Industrial Revolution*, Dublin, Repsol, 1978.

20. G. Hodgson, *The Democratic Economy*, Harmondsworth, Penguin, 1984, p. 164.

21. J. Freeman, F. Gaffikin and M. Morrissey, *Making The Economy Work: an alternative Strategy*, Belfast, ATGWU, Belfast, 1987, p. 53.

22. J. Lee, *Ireland 1912–1985*, p. 521.

23. E. O'Malley, *Industry and Economic Development*, p. 226.

24. Ibid, p.156.

25. J. Lee, *Ireland 1912–1985*, p. 535.

26. R. Crotty, *Farming Collapse: National Opportunity*, Dublin, Amarach, 1990, p. 1.

27. NIEC, *Economic Strategy in Northern Ireland*, Belfast, 1991, p. 1.

28. Bob Rowthorn, personal communication, August 1991.

29. NESC, *Ireland in the European Community*, Dublin 1989, p. 556.

30. NIEC, *Economic Strategy*, p. 56.

31. J. Lee, *Ireland 1912–1985*, p. 583.

32. See T. Lyne, 'Ireland, Northern Ireland and 1992: the barriers to technocratic anti-partitionism', *Public Administration*, 68, Winter 1990.

33. J. Lee, *Ireland 1912–1985*, p.631.

Select Bibliography

Allen. K. (1990) *Is Southern Ireland a Neo-Colony?*, Dublin, Bookmarks.

Bew, P. (1978) *Land and the National Question in Ireland 1858–1882*, Dublin, Gill and Macmillan.

Bloxham Maguire (1988) *Irish Economic and Financial Outlook – with a Special Summary of our Analysis on Ireland and the EEC Internal Market in 1992*, Dublin.

Breen, R. Hannan, D. Rottman, D. and Whelan, C. (1990) *Understanding Contemporary Ireland*, Basingstoke, Macmillan.

Callan, T., Nolan, B., Whelan, C. and Hannan, D. (1989) *Poverty, Welfare and Income in Ireland*, Dublin, ESRI.

Cecchini, P. (1988) *The European Challenge – 1992 – The Benefits of a Single Market*, London, Wildwood House.

Clancy, P., Drudy, S., Lynch, H. and O'Dowd, L. (eds) (1986) *Ireland: A Sociological Profile*, Dublin, Institute of Public Administration.

Commission of the European Communities (1987) *The Regions of the Enlarged Community: Third Periodic Report on the Social and Economic Situation and Development of the Regions of the Community*, Luxembourg, EC.

Coughlan, A. (1980), 'Ireland', in D. Seers and C. Vaitsos (eds) *Integration and Unequal Development: The Experience of the EEC*, London, Macmillan.

Crotty, R. (1986) *Ireland in Crisis: A Study in Capitalist Colonial Underdevelopment*, Dingle, Brandon.

Cullen, L.M. (ed.) (1976) *The Formation of the Irish Economy*, Cork, Mercier Press.

Cullen, L.M. (1972) *An Economic History of Ireland since 1600*, London, Batsford.

Culliton Report (1992) *A Time for Change: Industrial Policy for the 1990s: Report for the Industrial Policy Review Group*, Dublin, Stationery Office.

Daly, M. (1980) *A Social and Economic History of Ireland since 1800*, Dublin, The Educational Company.

Drudy, P.J. (1982) *Ireland: Land, Politics and People*, Cambridge, Cambridge University Press.

Economist Intelligence Unit (1988) *Ireland to 1992: Putting its House in Order*, London, EIU.

Girvin, B. (1989) *Between Two Worlds: Politics and Economy in Independent Ireland*, Dublin, Gill and MacMillan.

Grahl, J. and Teague, P. (1990) *1992: The Big Market*, London, Lawrence and Wishart.

Hainsworth, P. (1985) 'Northern Ireland in the European Community', in M. Keating and B. Jones (eds) *Regions in the European Community*, Oxford, Clarendon Press.

Harris, R., Jefferson, D. and Spencer, J. (eds) (1990) *The Northern Ireland Economy: A Comparative Study in the Economic Development of a Peripheral Region*, London, Longman.

Hart, J. (1985) 'The European Regional Development Fund and the Republic of Ireland', in M. Keating and B. Jones (eds) *Regions in the European Community*, Oxford, Clarendon Press.

Kennedy, K., Giblin, T. and McHugh, D. (1988) *The Economic Development of Ireland in the Twentieth Century*, London, Routledge.

Kennedy, K. and Ollerenshaw, P. (eds) (1985) *An Economic History of Ulster, 1820–1940*, Manchester, Manchester University Press.

Lee, J. (1989) *Ireland 1921–1985: Politics and Society*, Cambridge University Press.

Litton, E. (ed.) (1982) *Unequal Achievement: The Irish Experience 1957–1982*, Dublin, Institute of Public Administration.

Mokyr, J. (1985) *Why Ireland Starved: A Quantitative and Analytic History of the Irish Economy, 1800–1850*, London, Allen and Unwin.

Morrissey, H. (1989) *Women in Ireland: The Impact of 1992*, Belfast, Amalgamated Transport and General Workers Union.

NIEC and NESC (1988) *Economic Implications for Northern Ireland and the Republic of Ireland of Recent Developments in the European Community*, Northern Ireland Economic Council and National Economic and Social Council.

Northern Ireland Regional Development Plan (1989) London, HMSO.

O'Dowd, L. (1986) 'Beyond industrial society' in P. Clancy, S. Drudy, S. Lynch and L. Dowd (eds) *Ireland: a Sociological Profile*, Dublin, Institute of Public Administration.

O'Malley, E. (1989) *Industry and Economic Development: The Challenge of the Latecomer*, Dublin, Gill and Macmillan.

O'Neill, H. (1971) *Spatial Planning in the Small Economy: A Case Study of Ireland*, New York, Praegar.

O Siochru, J. (1988) *An Introduction to 1992 and its Implications for Trade Unions*, Dublin, SUS Research Ltd.

Rolston, M. and Tomlinson, M. (1988) *Unemployment in West Belfast: The Obair Report*, Belfast, Beyond the Pale Publications.

Rowthorn, B. and Wayne, N. (1988) *Northern Ireland: The Political Economy of Conflict*, Oxford, Polity Press.

SDLP (1988) *1992: The Implications of the Single Market for Northern Ireland*, Belfast, Social Democratic and Labour Party.

Seers, D. and Vaitsos, D. (1980) *Integration and Unequal Development: The Experience of the EEC*, London, Macmillan.

Sinn Fein/The Workers' Party (1978) *The Irish Industrial Revolution*, Dublin, Repsol.

Stanton, R. (1979) 'Foreign investment and host country politics: the Irish case', in D. Seers, B. Schaffer and M.L. Kiljunen (eds) *Under-Developed Europe*, Sussex, Harvester.

Teague, P. (1987) 'Multinational companies in the Northern Ireland economy: an outmoded model of industrial development', in P. Teague (ed.) *Beyond the Rhetoric: Politics, the Economy and Social Policy in Northern Ireland*, London, Lawrence and Wishart.

Wilson, T. (1989) *Ulster: Conflict and Consent*, Oxford, Basil Blackwell.

Index